Voices for Peace and Social Justice
Volume 3

By
Joseph Aprile

Joseph Aprile

Artwork by Joseph Aprile

Other Books by the Author

- Awakening from a Distant Dream – Novel
- At the Fringes of Experience – Collection of Novellas
- America and the Mythology of Greatness – Non-fiction
- Impaled on Time's Illustrious Arrow - Poetry
- The Surprising Latitude of Fate – Novel
- The Illusive Quality of Existence –Poetry
- The Human Equation –Short Stories
- A Particular Passing Through Time – Novel
- Voices for Peace and Social Justice – Non-Fiction
- Voices for Peace and Social Justice Volume II – Non-Fiction
- The Life and Times of Jeremy Sykes – Novel

- Daydreams and Other Lapses – Poetry
- The Human Equation Volume II – Short Stories & Essays
- Ode to Experience, Love, Truth and Time – Poetry
- Questions of Meaning in Matters of Philosophy and Science – Non-Fiction

Joseph Aprile

Table of Contents

Joseph Aprile

Introduction

The first volume in the Peace and Social Justice series was published in 2011 – ten years following the terrorist attack that destroyed the World Trade Center in New York City (September 11, 2001) and left thousands of innocent citizens dead and their families devastated.

Peace and Social Justice Volume II was published in 2014 at a time in human history when wars and civil strife were raging in Afghanistan, Syria and Iraq was still recovering from the Second Gulf War (2003 – 2011).

It is now 2022 and many examples of war and civil instability continue to plague the human world in places like Afghanistan and Syria. In addition, the Houthi peoples of Yemen are being ruthlessly assaulted by Saudi Arabia.

Yet another example of a minority ethnic population assaulted and brutally treated on account of their religious minority status are the Yezidi of Iraq – in Nineveh, Northern Iraq. They are a people besieged by the Islamic State of Iraq and Syria (ISIS). As a matter of fact one of the Yezidi women, Nadia Murad Basee Taha who was captured and enslaved managed to escape her imprisonment and has since been a courageous and outspoken advocate for her people and has been awarded the Nobel Peace Prize (2018). The full text of her acceptance speech is included in the section of this book devoted to her contributions to the cause of peace.

Authoritarian regimes remain very much in evidence in countries like Brazil, Russia, China, Hungary, and Saudi Arabia for example. These regimes use repressive methods to control their populations to ensure that power is retained in the hands of the few who possess it and to enforce a worldview that conforms to state-sanctioned goals. When this enforced set of imposed societal norms becomes decidedly incongruous to the tangible reality that its citizens and subjects actually experience, this disconnect inevitably leads to popular discord and unrest. Throughout human history, this essential reality has repeatedly contributed to the ultimate dissolution of empires.

The term "Failed States" has been coined to refer to those sovereignties that do not have the social, political, and economic infrastructure to support a system of codified laws, lack the organized agencies of government that typically unify a people and generally are extremely poor and bereft of economic power. Examples of failed states include – Yemen, Somalia, South Sudan, Democratic Republic Congo, Central African Republic, Chad, and Sudan. Lacking a cohesive central government, these failed states become vulnerable to exploitation by more powerful neighbors and by internal civil strife and war. This is nothing new in terms of the human condition. These kinds of unbalanced relationships between powerful and weak nations have been evident throughout the expanse of human history, for nation states continue to be driven by self-interest that often does not conform to the needs of their people and are more aligned with the priorities of wealth and power.

Although there are many progressive movements evident throughout the world whose purpose is to achieve a greater measure of peace and social justice, there is also the troubling evidence of the growth of fascism in many parts of the world.

This reality was made particularly evident in the United States with the meteoric rise of the Presidency of Donald Trump (2016-2020) a grossly incompetent holder of this office who unabashedly promoted a xenophobic worldview and who used the "big lie" as a way to manipulate and direct his following. While in office, his boisterous and often mean-spirited polemics embraced a so-called "America First" political philosophy that particularly targeted a receptive white and male disaffected audience. His obvious contempt for democratic principles and the rule of law was made evident by his failed attempt on January 6, 2020 to direct an unruly mob to the nation's capital with the intent of subverting the peaceful transition of power after he had clearly lost the Presidential election of 2020 – an outcome that he had repeatedly claimed, was "rigged" without any real evidence to support this assertion.

Fascism ascribes to the idea of racial and ethnic superiority, and for this reason has some appeal to those who have come to feel threatened by the realities of the twenty-first century that embrace a more global, diverse, and inclusive world view. Fascism, by its nature, is extremist in terms of its philosophical constructs and is inherently dangerous, for it promotes violent behavior directed against racial and ethnic minorities and views any divergence from the imposed norm as contemptible and worthy of severe punishment.

There are currently 7.9 billion people (2022) populating the planet Earth. Science has clearly and unambiguously demonstrated that there are no real and substantial differences between any members of the human species other than those unique attributes that we all possess. In this light, race is a patently artificial and decidedly false construct.

Yet, in spite of this intrinsic reality, the human world is consumed by hatreds and antagonisms born of these manufactured differences. It seems that racial, ethnic, religious, cultural, and political differences represent the driving force for violence and aggression between and within nations. Peace remains an elusive goal for humanity.

Unlike in the past, however, there is an additional and disturbing reality that overshadows humanity's prospects for the future and that is the prospect of the calamitous impact of climate change as a consequence of the unabated use of fossil fuels to drive industrialization since the beginning of the 18th century. This a global issue that needs concerted action on the part of all nations. For this reason, it is imperative that peace and social justice be achieved between all peoples so that global problems like climate change can be effectively recognized, and remedies devised to ensure a stable and prosperous future for the coming generations.

Thankfully, there are many individuals, groups, and collectives that are directing their energies towards creating a future more aligned with peace and social justice. In this volume, twenty-eight individuals are celebrated for their contribution to this over-arching goal. These individuals have been grouped into the following categories.

- Individuals of historic Importance include Anne Hutchinson, Chief Joseph of the Nez Perce, George Washington Williams, Dame Cecily Saunders, William Wilberforce, Ann Arnold Hedgeman, and Emma Gotcher
- Contemporary leaders involved in the American Civil Rights movement include John Louis, Walter Ahmann, Stacey Abrams, Arthur Waskow, Phyllis Berman, and Pramila Jayapal
- The category that specifically refers to the U.S. Internment of Japanese-Americans during World War II includes Fred Koramatsu, Gordon Hirabyashi and Walt and Milly Woodward.
- Those involved in regional human rights issues around the globe include Nadia Murad Basee Taha of Iraq, Rose Mapendo of

the Democratic Republic of Congo, Dr, Denis Mukwege Mukengere of the Democratic Republic of Congo, Raif Badawi of Saudi Arabia, Jacinda Ardern of New Zealand, and Oscar Arias Sanchez of Costa Rica.

- And finally individuals involved in Native People's Rights includes Chief Raoni Metuktire, Eloise P. Cobell, Maxima Acuna De Chaupe, Sarah Deer and Cecile Ann Hansen.

Collectively, these individuals have made many contributions to the overarching goal of making significant progress towards a more peaceful world in which equality and social justice can blossom and thrive. What follows is an examination of the nature and extent of their efforts.

Arthur Waskow and Phyllis Berman

Arthur Waskow is the founder of the highly recognized and acclaimed Shalom Center (theshalomcenter.org). Waskow was born in 1933 and spent his young life in Baltimore, Maryland. As a young man he received his undergraduate degree at Johns Hopkins and eventually a doctorate in United States History at the University of Wisconsin at Madison (1963). At the time of his graduation, the United States was in the midst of social and political turmoil revolving around two distinct and momentous issues - the Vietnam War and the Civil Rights Movement.

From 1959 to 1961, during his academic studies, he was passionately involved in nuclear weapons disarmament and civil-rights in his role as a legislative assistant for U.S. Congressman Robert Krastenmeier of Wisconson. From 1961 to 1963, he was a Senior Fellow of the Peace Research

Institute. This work inspired him to help create the Institute for Policy Studies and acted as a Fellow there until 1977.

Throughout the troubling era of the sixties, Waskow was a vociferous and relentless advocate for world peace and non-violent action against social injustice. He wrote extensively on these issues including literally hundreds of articles and many books. In 1968, he was a part of the Washington D.C. delegation to the Democratic National Convention of 1968.

Waskow's interests eventually extended to the use of renewable energy and energy conservation – he began to understand the dangers to humanity of the ongoing reality of climate change. His activism in regard to this issue took the form of his role as a Fellow of the Public Resource Center in Washington D.C.

Although his dedication to social activism remained intact, in 1969, he turned his attention to Jewish life in America. At the time, he felt it needed spiritual renewal. The passion he had for this new direction he embarked upon is reflected in his Haggadah (a traditional Passover text) entitled, *The Freedom Seder*.

The following excerpts from this masterful peace, show how Waskow incorporated the modern struggle for peace and social justice into the body of a traditional Jewish text in celebration of the Passover –

"For as one of the greatest of our prophets, whose own death by violence at a time near the Passover were member in tears tonight as the prophet Martin Luther King called us to know: "The old law of an eye for an eye leaves everybody blind. It destroys community and makes brotherhood impossible. It creates bitterness in the survivors and brutality in the destroyers. But the principle of nonviolent resistance seeks to reconcile the truths of two opposites-acquiescence and violence. The nonviolent resister rises to the noble height of opposing the unjust system while loving the perpetrators of the system. Nonviolence can reach men where the law cannot touch them. So, we will match your capacity to inflict suffering with our capacity to endure suffering. We will not hate you, but we cannot in all good conscience obey your unjust laws. And in winning our freedom we will so appeal to your heart and conscience that we will win you in the process.

"And as rabbi Buber said, "The revolutionary lives on the knife's edge. The question that harasses him is not merely the moral or religious one of whether he may kill; his quandary has nothing at all to do with selling his soul to the devil' in order to bring the revolution to victory. His entanglement in the situation is here just the tension between end and means. I cannot conceive anything real corresponding to the saying that the end sanctifies the means; but I mean something which is real in the highest sense of the term when I say that the means profane, actually make meaningless, the end, that is, its realization! What is realized is the farther from the goal that was set, the more out of accord with it is the method by which it was realized. The ensuring of the revolution may only drain its heart's blood.

"Or as the rabbi Hannah Arendt wrote, "Man the political being is endowed with the power of speech. Speech is helpless when confronted with violence. Violence itself is incapable of speech. When violence rules absolutely, not only the laws but everything and everybody must fall silent.

"But even the prophet Gandhi, who made his life a call to nonviolent revolution, warned his people, "Where there is only a choice between cowardice and violence, I would advise violence. Unless you feel that in nonviolence you have come into possession of a force infinitely superior to the one you have and in the use of which you are adept, you should have nothing to do with non-violence and resume the arms you possessed before.

"So, the struggles for freedom that remain will be more formidable and difficult than any we have met so far. For we must struggle for a freedom that enfolds stern justice, stern bravery, and stern love. Blessed art thou, 0 Lord our God! who hast confronted us with the necessity of choice and of creating our own book of thy Law. How many and how hard are the choices and the tasks the Almighty has set before us!

"For if we were to end a single genocide but not to stop the other wars that kill men and women as we sit here, it would not be sufficient.

"If we were to end those bloody wars but not disarm the nations of the weapons that could destroy all mankind, it would not be sufficient.

"If we were to disarm the nations but not to end the brutality with which the police attack black people in some countries, brown people in others; Moslems in some countries, Hindus in other; Baptists in some countries, atheists in others; Communists in some countries, conservatives in other it would not be sufficient.

"If we were to end outright police brutality but not prevent some people from wallowing in luxury while others starved, it would not be sufficient.

"If we were to make sure that no one starved but were not to free the daring poets from their jails, it would not be sufficient.

"If we were to free the poets from their jails but to train the minds of people so that they could not understand the poets, it would not be sufficient.

"If we educated all men and women to understand the free creative poets but forbade them to explore their own inner ecstasies, it would not be sufficient.

"If we allowed men and women to explore their inner ecstasies but would not allow them to love one another and share in the human fraternity, it would not be sufficient.

"How much then are we in duty bound to struggle, work, share, give, think, plan, feel, organize, sit-in, speak out, hope, and be on behalf of Mankind! For we must end the genocide [in Vietnam], stop the bloody wars that are killing men and women as we sit here, disarm the nations of the deadly weapons that threaten to destroy us all, end the brutality with which the police beat minorities in many countries, make sure that no one starves, free the poets from their jails, educate us all to understand their poetry, allow us all to explore our inner ecstasies, and encourage and aid us to love one another and share in the human fraternity. All these!"

In 1982, he became a member of the faculty of the Reconstructionist Rabbinical College, and in 1983 he co-founded the Shalom Center. The Shalom Center's mission is to revitalize modern Judaism. In keeping with this mission, it works closely with the National Council of Churches, Muslim groups and has aligned itself with teachers and activists in order to find common approaches to world problems including racism, poverty, climate change, the Israeli-Palestine conflict etc.

Rabbi Arthur Waskow works tirelessly in the pursuit of peace and social justice. His generosity of spirit is an inspiration to all of those who desire a more peaceful and equitable human world

Phyllis Berman

Phyllis Berman (Wife of Arthur Waskow) was born in 1942. Berman is the founder of the Riverside Language Program in New York City. This program was designed to introduce adult immigrants and refugees to the English language through an intensive approach. This program was begun in 1979, and Berman was its director until 2016.

In addition, she is a teacher and religious leader within the Jewish Renewal Movement. She has been an advocate and activist for immigrant rights and has been arrested for her participation in non-violent protests regarding her support for the immigrant and refugee populations.

Berman has been deeply involved in the Jewish Renewal movement. According to the Alliance for Jewish Renewal (ALEPH — aleph.org) the Jewish Renewal movement is defined in the following way,

"Jewish Renewal is a trans-denominational approach to revitalizing Judaism.

"We combine the socially progressive values of egalitarianism, the joy of Hasidism, the informed do-it-yourself spirit of the havurah movement, and the accumulated wisdom of centuries of tradition.

"We value deep ecumenism; in Hillel's words, we learn from every person and spiritual tradition.

"We create innovative, accessible, and welcoming prayer experiences.

"We shape halacha (Jewish law) into a living way of walking in the world.

"And we seek to deepen the ongoing, joyful, and fundamental connection, with a God who connects us all, which is at the heart of Jewish practice.

"Renewal is an attitude, not a denomination, and offers tools to all branches of Judaism, including:

"An emphasis on accessible spiritual experience.

"Contemplative practices (Jewish Renewal teachers were the first to recover meditative practices from the dusty attic of Jewish tradition, and to return them to their rightful place as central Jewish spiritual technologies);

"Davvenology, the art and practice of being a living laboratory for creative and renewed Jewish prayer, in modalities including chant and embodied prayer;

"Sage-ing, trainings and tools for rethinking aging as a journey of unearthing wisdom;

"Hashpa'ah (spiritual direction) as a tool for unpacking the holy potential of every moment and for discerning the voice of God.

"Renewal seeks to balance forward-thinking with backward-compatibility. We know we can't drive if we're only looking in the rear-view mirror, but neither can we move forward if we don't know where we've been."

Berman's specific roles within the Jewish Renewal movement have been as Director of the Summer Program of the Elat Chayyim Center for Healing and Renewal, co-leading retreats for the Awakened Heart Project, and teaching at ALEPH kallot (retreat). She was ordained as a Rabbi in 2003.

As a team, Rabbi Berman and her husband Rabbi Arthur Waskow (see above) have co-authored a number of books including, *Tales of Tikkun, Jewish Stories to Heal the Wounded World*, and *Freedom Journeys*. They have made a significant contribution towards a further broadening of understanding between peoples of differing spiritual values and religious backgrounds. This is of special importance in a human world beset by animosity and suspicion.

Walt and Milly Woodward

On February 19, 1942, the executive order (EO) 9066 was promulgated by President Franklin D. Roosevelt. The following is the full text of this executive order –

"Authorizing the Secretary of War to Prescribe Military Areas

"Whereas the successful prosecution of the war requires every possible protection against espionage and against sabotage to national-defense material, national-defense premises, and national-defense utilities as defined in Section 4, Act of April 20, 1918, 40 Stat. 533, as amended by the Act of November 30, 1940, 54 Stat. 1220, and the Act of August 21, 1941, 55 Stat. 655 (U.S.C., Title 50, Sec. 104).

"Now, therefore, by virtue of the authority vested in me as President of the United States, and Commander in Chief of the Army and Navy, I hereby authorize and direct the Secretary of War, and the Military Commanders whom he may from time to time designate, whenever he or any designated Commander deems such action necessary or desirable, to prescribe military areas in such places and of such extent as he or the appropriate Military Commander may determine, from which any or all persons may be excluded, and with respect to which, the right of any person to enter, remain in, or leave shall be subject to whatever restrictions the Secretary of War or the appropriate Military Commander may impose in his discretion. The Secretary of War is hereby authorized to provide for residents of any such area who are excluded therefrom, such transportation, food, shelter, and other accommodations as may be necessary, in the judgment of the Secretary of War or the said Military Commander, and until other arrangements are made, to accomplish the purpose of this order. The designation of military areas in any region or locality shall supersede designations of prohibited and restricted areas by the Attorney General under the Proclamations of December 7 and 8, 1941, and shall supersede the responsibility and authority of the Attorney General under the said Proclamations in respect of such prohibited and restricted areas.

"I hereby further authorize and direct the Secretary of War and the said Military Commanders to take such other steps as he or the appropriate Military Commander may deem advisable to enforce compliance with the restrictions applicable to each Military area here in above authorized to be designated, including the use of Federal troops and other Federal Agencies, with authority to accept assistance of state and local agencies.

"I hereby further authorize and direct all Executive Departments, independent establishments and other Federal Agencies, to assist the Secretary of War or the said Military Commanders in carrying out this Executive Order, including the furnishing of medical aid, hospitalization, food, clothing, transportation, use of land, shelter, and other supplies, equipment, utilities, facilities, and services.

"This order shall not be construed as modifying or limiting in any way the authority heretofore granted under Executive Order (EO) No. 8972, dated December 12, 1941, nor shall it be construed as limiting or modifying the duty and responsibility of the Federal Bureau of Investigation, with respect to the investigation of alleged acts of sabotage or the duty and responsibility of the Attorney General and the Department of Justice under the Proclamations of December 7 and 8, 1941, prescribing regulations for the conduct and control of alien enemies, except as such duty and responsibility is superseded by the designation of military areas here under."

In effect, all Japanese-Americans were ordered to vacate their places of residence and business and move en masse into concentration camps setup up to accommodate them. This occurred in the midst of World War II after the Japanese bombing of Pearl Harbor. Although the United States was already at war with Nazi Germany, no such mandate was imposed upon the many German-Americans living throughout the country.

This mass evacuation imposed a severe burden on the lives of those citizens who were forced to abandon their homes and properties for the "duration" of the war.

In 1940, Walt and Milly Woodward from Bainbridge, Washington purchased the weekly publication, the *Bainbridge Review*. Two months before the Japanese attack on Pearl Harbor (December 7, 1941) that precipitated the declaration of war against Japan, they pledged in a front-page editorial to, "strive to speak the truth, unafraid. whether it be on a national interest or something purely local."

They lived up to this promise to their readership; for, the day following the Japanese attack on Pearl Harbor, they warned that, "There is a danger of a blind, wild hysterical hatred of all persons who can trace ancestry to Japan. That some of those persons happen to be American citizens...easily could be swept away by mob hysteria." They attempted to raise the awareness of their subscribers to the loyalty of their Japanese-American fellow citizens by stating in their newspaper that, "These Japanese Americans of ours haven't bombed anybody...They have given every indication of loyalty to this nation. They have sent their own sons – six of them – into the United States Army."

As a result of EO 8972, 272 Japanese Americans were forced to abandon their homes, properties and friendships and were moved to Manzanar – one of the ten Japanese concentrations that were erected throughout the nation. Manzanar was located at the foot of the Sierra Nevada mountains in California's Owens Valley that ultimately housed 10,000 individuals.

This courageous and tenacious couple continued to speak out throughout the war regarding the injustice of this forced and massive relocation. As a matter of fact, their publication was the only newspaper throughout the entire country to take such an unpopular position. The Woodwards actually hired high school students – Paul Ohtaki, Sa Nakata, Tony Koura and Sada Omoto to report from Manzanar on the daily lives and challenges facing the inmates of that camp.

After the war, Walt and Milly Woodward remained strong local activists of the Bainbridge Island community especially in regard to local schools, construction of a new library and public transportation. Walt ultimately stepped down as editor of the Review in 1963; the newspaper was sold in 1988. Walt worked for a time on the editorial board of the Seattle times. Milly returned to her career as a high school teacher and died in 1989. Walt passed away in 2001 at the age ninety-one.

Walt and Milly Woodward were recognized posthumously by the Asian Journalists Association for their outspoken opposition to the involuntary internment of

Japanese-Americans. They were recipients of the Special Recognition Award.

Finally, on March 30, 2009 (the sixty-seventh anniversary of the internment), the ground-breaking ceremony took place to begin construction of the Bainbridge Island Japanese American Exclusion Memorial to honor those Japanese-Americans of Bainbridge Island who were moved into concentration camps.

William Wilberforce

William Wilberforce, born in August of 1759, was a powerful advocate for the abolition of slavery in the then extensive British Empire. Great Britain's involvement in the promulgation of slavery was, for the most part, driven by economic and commercial interests that spanned the globe. The industrial revolution that began in England, was essentially financed by its colonial activities that embraced slavery.

Wilberforce was born into a wealthy and influential family in Hull, in the East Riding of Yorkshire, England. Following his father's untimely death in 1768, his mother sent her nine-year old son to his affluent uncle and aunt who had residences at St. James' Place, London, and

Wimbledon. He eventually became very attached to his "new" family. His mother, however, was a member of England's traditional Anglican Church and was concerned about her son's exposure to Evangelical Christianity and had him return to her at the age of 12. It was his Aunt Hannah who was especially influential in this regard.

At eighteen years of age (1777), Wilberforce attended St. John's College in Cambridge University. He was not an exceptional student; he already had an inheritance and was not particularly motivated. However, while studying at St. John's College he became close friends with William Pitt who would later become Prime Minister (1783-1801 and 1804-1806). Nearing the end of his stay at Cambridge, Wilberforce decided to run for Parliament and won a seat at the age of 21 as an independent.

While he was in Parliament, he distinguished himself as an eloquent speaker. There, he met James Ramsay in 1783 and for the first time, he was exposed to the subject of slavery. The Reverend James Ramsay (1733 – 1789) was a ship's surgeon, Anglican priest, and was a leader in the abolitionist movement. This relationship signaled a significant change in Wilberforce's overall worldview. Between 1784 and 1786, Wilberforce seemed to have experienced an intense religious conversion. As a result, he was tempted to abandon his political ambitions; however, his good friend and mentor John Newton encouraged him to use his political position to push for social reform. John Newton was an Anglican clergyman and former slave ship master who eventually spoke out against the slave trade. In 1789, Wilberforce witnessed his country's loss of the American Colonies after its defeat in the American Revolutionary War. This may have impressed upon him the reality of a shrinking British Empire as further encouragement for the need for major reform.

Using his new-found religious conviction, Wilberforce began to lead, guided by conscience. The slave trade and the abhorrent character of slavery inspired him to become a forceful advocate for the abolition of slavery and the slave trade. He was encouraged by Sir Charles Middleton to represent the cause in Parliament. Charles Middleton was a British Royal Naval officer who, in his later years, played a critical role in the abolition of the slave trade in the British Empire. He was also influenced by the writings of Rev. James Ramsay (as mentioned earlier). Furthermore, in 1787, Wilberforce was introduced to Thomas Clarkson who gave him a copy of his treatise on slavery entitled, *Essay on Slavery*. They joined together in a collaborative effort to abolish the slave trade that lasted nearly a half of a century.

The following is Wilberforce's impassioned speech in support of the abolition of slavery to the Parliament in 1789 in its entirety –

"When I consider the magnitude of the subject which I am to bring before the House—a subject, in which the interests, not of this country, nor of Europe alone, but of the whole world, and of posterity, are involved: and when I think, at the same time, on the weakness of the advocate who has undertaken this great cause—when these reflections press upon my mind, it is impossible for me not to feel both terrified and concerned at my own inadequacy to such a task. But when I reflect, however, on the encouragement which I have had, through the whole course of a long and laborious examination of this question, and how much candor I have experienced, and how conviction has increased within my own mind, in proportion as I have advanced in my labours;—when I reflect, especially, that however averse any gentleman may now be, yet we shall all be of one opinion in the end;—when I turn myself to these thoughts, I take courage—I determine to forget all my other fears, and I march forward with a firmer step in the full assurance that my cause will bear me out, and that I shall be able to justify upon the clearest principles, every resolution in my hand, the avowed end of which is, the total abolition of the slave trade. I wish exceedingly, in the outset, to guard both myself and the House from entering into the subject with any sort of passion. It is not their passions I shall appeal to—I ask only for their cool and impartial reason; and I wish not to take them by surprise, but to deliberate, point by point, upon every part of this question. I mean not to accuse anyone, but to take the shame upon myself, in common, indeed, with the whole parliament of Great Britain, for having suffered this horrid trade to be carried on under their authority. We are all guilty - we ought all to plead guilty, and not to exculpate ourselves by throwing the blame on others; and I therefore deprecate every kind of reflection against the various descriptions of people who are more immediately involved in this wretched business. Having now disposed of the first part of this subject, I must speak of the transit of the slaves in the West Indies. This I confess, in my own opinion, is the most wretched part of the whole subject. So much misery condensed in so little room, is more than the human imagination had ever before conceived. I will not accuse the Liverpool merchants: I will allow them, nay, I will believe them to be men of humanity; and I will therefore believe, if it were not for the enormous magnitude and extent of the evil which distracts their attention from individual cases, and makes them think generally, and therefore less feelingly on the subject, they would never have persisted in the trade. I verily believe therefore, if the William Wilberforce's 1789 Abolition Speech National History Day 2007 61 wretchedness of any one of the many hundred Negroes stowed in each ship could be brought before their view, and remain within the sight of the African Merchant, that there is no one among them whose heart would bear it. Let anyone imagine to himself 6 or 700 of these wretches chained two and two, surrounded with every object that is nauseous and disgusting, diseased, and struggling under every kind of wretchedness! How can we bear to think of such a scene as this? One would think it had been determined to heap upon them all the varieties of bodily pain, for the purpose of blunting the feelings of the mind; and yet, in this very point (to show the power of human prejudice) the situation of the slaves has been described by Mr. Norris, one of the Liverpool delegates, in a manner which, I am sure will convince the House how interest can draw a film across the eyes, so thick, that total blindness could do no more; and how it is our duty therefore to trust not to the reasonings of interested men, or to their way of colouring a transaction... As soon as ever I had arrived thus far in my investigation of the slave trade, I confess to you sir, so enormous so dreadful, so irremediable did its wickedness appear that my own mind was completely made up for the abolition. A trade founded in iniquity, and carried on as this was, must be abolished, let the policy be what it might - let the consequences be what they would, I from this time determined that I would never rest till I had effected its abolition."

After years of concerted effort during which time public sentiment in favor of abolition grew, Wilberforce put forth a bill called the *Slave Trade Act* that made it illegal for slave owners to participate in the trading of slaves with the French colonies. Although this bill fell short of an entire ban on the slave trade, it reduced the slave trade by 75% - it was a masterful piece of legislation. It became law in 1807.

However, the battle was not yet won. Finally, in 1833, the *Slavery Abolition Act* was passed. This act made slavery illegal in most parts of the Empire. Just three days after this monumental reform in British law and custom, Wilberforce died on July 29, 1833.

Without Wilberforce's persistent and undaunted efforts to end the support of slavery In the British Empire, it probably would not have happened in such a timely fashion. It would take some thirty years before President Abraham Lincoln issued the *Emancipation Proclamation* (January 1,

1863) that ended slavery in the United States in the midst of the disastrous American Civil War.

Nadia Murad Basee Taha

Nadia Murad Basee Taha (Murad), was born in 1993 in the village of Kocho in Sinjar, Iraq. Her family members are part of the Yazidi ethno-religious minority. Their livelihood was faming. The Yazidis have come into focus and captured the world's attention on account of the fact that the Islamic State of Iraq and Syria (ISIS) has made repeated attempts to annihilate them. It has been estimated that there are some 700,000 members of this community living in the countries of Iraq, Armenia and Georgia and other parts of the world. Murad has become an international voice of conscience in regard to her peoples' plight. The vast majority of the Yazidis reside in northern Iraq around Mt. Sinjar (see image below).

<u>Who are the Yazidis?</u>

As mentioned earlier, estimates put the global number of Yazidis at around 700,000 people, with the vast majority of them concentrated in northern Iraq, in and around Sinjar. The following description is derived from a report that appeared in The Guardian in August of 2014 authored by Raya Jalabi.

"A historically misunderstood group, the Yazidis are predominantly ethnically Kurdish, and have kept alive their syncretic religion for centuries, despite many years of oppression and threatened extermination.

"The ancient religion is rumoured to have been founded by an 11th century Ummayyad sheikh and is derived from Zoroastrianism (an ancient Persian faith founded by the philosopher Zoroaster (~630 – 550 BC). The religion has taken elements from Christianity and Islam ranging from baptism (Christianity) to circumcision (Islam) to reverence of fire as a manifestation from God (derived from Zoroastrianism) and yet remains distinctly non-Abrahamic.   This derivative quality has contributed to regarding the Yazidis as belonging to a sect.

"At the core of the Yazidis' marginalization is their worship of a fallen angel, Melek Tawwus, or Peacock Angel, one of the seven angels that take primacy in their beliefs. Unlike the fall from grace of Satan, in the Judeo-Christian tradition, Melek Tawwus was forgiven and returned to heaven by God. The importance of Melek Tawwus to the Yazidis has given them an undeserved reputation for being devil-worshippers – a notoriety that, in the climate of extremism gripping Iraq, has turned life-threatening.

"Under Ottoman rule in the 18th and 19th centuries alone, the Yazidis were subject to 72 genocidal massacres. More recently in 2007, hundreds of Yazidis were killed as a spate of car bombs ripped through their stronghold in northern Iraq. With numbers of dead as close to 800, according to the Iraqi Red Crescent, this was one of the single deadliest events to take place during the American-led invasion.

"The Yazidis had been denounced as infidels by Al-Qaida in Iraq, a predecessor of Isis, which sanctioned their indiscriminate killing."

ISIS fighters invaded the village of Kocho where Murad was a student. She was nineteen years old at the time when she witnessed the massacre that followed resulting in the death of 600 inhabitants including six of Murad's brothers and step-brothers. The younger women were forced into slavery. She was one of 6,700 women taken prisoner by ISIS. As a prisoner she was beaten, tortured, and raped when she made a failed attempt to escape her captors.

Murad ultimately did escape when her captor unwittingly left the door unlocked in the house where she was imprisoned. She was eventually smuggled out of ISIS-controlled territory and was safely transported to a refugee camp in the neighboring town of Duhok. In February of 2015, she gave her first testimony of her horrific ordeal to reporters. Murad moved to Germany, taking advantage of a refugee program sponsored by the German Government.

The following, is the statement Murad made to the UN Security Council on December 18, 2015 -

"Mr. President:

"Ladies and gentlemen, Delegates of the Security Council, Good afternoon.

"I would like to thank United States for calling for this debate and for inviting me to speak.

"It is with great sadness, gratitude and hope that I stand before you today as one of the few survivors of one of the world's oldest ethnic and religious group now threatened by extinction.

"I am here today to speak on the way the so-called Islamic State trafficked us, transformed the Yazidi women into Sex slaves, and the way IS committed a genocide against my people. I am here to tell what has happened to me and my community that lost hope is headed to the unknown, I am here also to speak on behalf of those who remain in captivity.

"I am here to speak about a global terrorist organization that came to end our existence, culture and freedom, to speak about the nightmare that change life for a community overnight.

"Before August 3, 2014, I was living with my family in Kocho village with my single mother and brothers and sisters, our village was beautiful, we were living in peace. But on August 3rd, the militants of the Islamic State, attacked our areas and we found ourselves faced with a brutal genocide. These large groups of armed men of various nationalities in uniforms with weapons, had decided that the Yazidis were infidels and had to be eradicated.

"The Islamic State didn't come to kill the women and girls, but to use us as spoils of war, as objects to be sold with little or to be gifted for free.

"Their cruelty was not merely opportunistic. The IS soldiers came with a pre-established policy to commit such crimes.

"Islamic State had one intention, to destroy the Yazidi identity by force, rape, recruitment of children, and destruction of holy sites they captured, especially against the Yazidi woman where they used rape as a mean of destruction for Yazidi women and girls and ensuring these women will never return to a normal life.

"On August 15th, the Militants called us to the school building, where they separated men from us; I witnessed from the second floor of the school, they took the men and killed them, including 6 of my brothers and stepbrothers who were killed, and 3 who escaped the mass killing with Creator Blessing.

"We, the women and the children, were driven away to another area. Along the way, they insulted us, they were forcefully touching women and girls.

"I was taken with some other 150 girls to Mosul, in a building in Mosul, there were thousands of Yazidis women and children and who were previously captured by ISIL to be offered as gifts.

"A militant approached me, he said they would take me, I was looking down, I was terrified, when I looked up, I saw a big man, he looked like a minister. I cried, I said I won't want you, I told him you are too big for me, I am a little girl. Another militant walked in, I was still looking down, I saw his feet, he had small feet, I begged him to take me for himself, I was so scared from the big militant.

"The one who took me asked me to convert, I did not, he then one day asked me for "marriage", I told him I am sick, most of the captive women there had their menstrual period due to the fears. Then he one day forced me to dress for him and put make up, I did, and in that black night, he did it.

"He forced me to serve his militant squad, he insulted me by forcing me to dress improperly. And I was unable to bear more rape and torture, I decided to escape, but I failed and I was captured by the guards.

"That night, he beat me up, forced to undress, and put me in a room with 6 militants. They continued to commit crimes to my body until I became unconscious.

"After three months of abduction, finally I was able to escape. Now I live in Germany. Thanks to Germany who accepted to treat me.

"But it was not only me who suffered, it was a collective suffering, The Islamic State gave us two choices, covert of die, for those who accepted to convert fearing their lives, their men were killed, women were enslaved and children were recruited.

"To date, 16 mass graves have been found, including a mass grave of 80 women who they didn't desire, therefore decided to kill. More than 400,000 Yazidis are displaced, more than 40 percent of our areas remain under control of IS, and the liberated areas are not habitable because of the destruction and Yazidi fears to return and live in their homes with peace.

"Over the past week only, more than 70 Yazidi women and children drowned on their way through dangerous paths to Europe, thousands are seeking an exit, a great percentage see immigration in the only choice.

"Mrs. President, Ladies and gentlemen:

"The Islamic State have made the Yazidi women a fuel for human trafficking.

"I am presenting to you our requests and I have hope that humanity has not died, yet:

1.   Bring back more than 3400 women and children currently suffering under the mercy of those who lost every bit of mercy.

2.   Recognize the mass killing, enslavement and human trafficking committed as a genocide, I appeal to you to find a way to open a case before the International Criminal Court.

3.   Liberate our land, Liberate Kocho so that Kocho people can bury the remains of their dead, provide Yazidi Areas and other threatened minorities areas with international protection so we can return one day and live in peace, I also request that you allocate an international fund to compensate victims and build our areas.

4.   Open your borders for my community, we are victims of a genocide and we have the right to seek a safe place where our dignity will be preserved. We request that to give Yazidis and other threatened minorities the choice to resettle, especially to the victims of human trafficking, as Germany Did.

5.   Bring an End to ISIL, I have seen them, I have lived the pain they caused. We have to bring all human traffickers criminals and those who committed a genocide to justice so that the women and children in Nigeria, Syria, Somalia, and everywhere in the world can live in peace. These crimes against women and their freedom shall stop now."

This statement paints a compelling and moving story of the experiences of a young woman and is an indictment of the abhorrent and extremist behavior of those who are apparently "possessed" by a fanatical ideology that sanctions such unimaginable brutality in the name of religious belief. It also illustrates the remarkable persistence, courage, and strength of character of Murad in the light of her horrendous experiences in her native Iraq.

Rose Mapendo

Rose Mapendo was born in Mulenge within the Democratic Republic of the Congo (DRC) in 1963. She was a member of the Banyamulenge Tutsi tribe. Mapendo grew up in a Christian household. As is customary for women in her culture, she was married at the young age of sixteen years. In 1994, she moved to the city of Mbuji-Mayi where her husband could successfully pursue his career as a butcher, and her children could go to school.

These plans, however, were severely disrupted with the outbreak of mass killings of the Tutsi people that began in neighboring Rwanda. On April 7, 1994, members of the Rwandan army murdered ten Belgian peacekeepers as part of strategy to eliminate the Tutsi people from Rwanda. In three short months, the Hutu- led government of Rwanda, killed an estimated one-half to a million innocent civilian Tutsis. This madness ultimately spread to the DRC. Mapendo and her family attempted to hide from the invading troops but were eventually found and captured.

They were taken to a prison camp on the night of September 23, 1998

She remained in that camp for sixteen months. Her existence there is hard to imagine. The government ordered the extra-judicial killing of all the men; Mapendo's husband was among them. The camp lacked sanitation, medical care and the food provided was woefully inadequate. During this time, Mapendo was pregnant with twins. In order to save her own life, she was coerced into giving her seventeen-year-old daughter to a soldier for sex. Mapendo managed to give birth under abysmal conditions and tied and cut the umbilical cords with a piece of wood. She wisely named her newborns after two of the camp's commanders. This strategy ultimately saved her life: for, when orders from the government came to have the prisoners executed, one of the commanders had her and her family transferred to another prison facility in Kinshasa, capital of the DRC. Within weeks they were delivered to a human rights center and ultimately to a Red Cross center in Cameroon through an American effort to resettle Tutsi refugees.

Finally, in 2000, Mapendo and her children received refugee status and settled in the United States. In 2007, she received word that her daughter was alive, and Nangabire ultimately rejoined her family in the U.S.

Once securing the safety of herself and family, Mapendo could certainly have chosen to quietly pursue her new life. However, this is not what she chose to do. Instead, she chose the path of forgiveness and women's empowerment. She felt compelled to tell her story. As a result, the public broadcasting system (PBS) broadcasted a documentary entitled, *Pushing the Elephant* that describes Mapendo's mission and personal experiences culminating in the reunion with her daughter.

The following are audio excerpts from that film (hosted by Michel Martin) –

"And now we meet a remarkable woman. Her name is Rose Mapendo. She was the 2009 United Nations Humanitarian of the Year. She is from the Democratic Republic of Congo. She is an advocate for global health and women's empowerment and a mother to 10 children. But those words don't really capture her story, which is both remarkable and all too common. That story is told in a new documentary called "Pushing the Elephant." It premiered this week as part of the PBS series "Independent Lens."

"And, again, I have to say that this conversation does touch on the issue of sexual violence and thus might not be suitable for all listeners. With that being said, Rose Mapendo is with us from Tempe, Arizona. Welcome, thank you so much for joining us.

Ms. ROSE MAPENDO (2009 United Nations Humanitarian of the Year): Thank you, Michel.

MARTIN: The documentary tells your story of surviving the violence that your family encountered during what many people call the African world war. Certainly, living through those events had to have been incredibly painful. I must tell you that watching the film is painful. But recounting those events time and again must also be painful. And I wanted to ask why you were willing to do it.

Ms. MAPENDO: First of all, it is to raise the awareness and to tell a story of the innocent people. And I truly believe I just survive for reason. It was a choice for me to be a voice even though I knew nobody will change my past. Because I think the people can learn from the past to fix the present.

MARTIN: Just to some of the things that you lived through, which are recounted in the documentary, at the time that your community was invaded, your husband was killed, you were captured with how many children at the time? Seven, at that time. Correct?

Ms. MAPENDO: Yes.

MARTIN: You were separated from one child. And while you were imprisoned in, really, what can only be called a death camp, women and children were really just kept there to die with terrible conditions. You found that you were pregnant with twins and this presented a terrible dilemma, not just because the conditions that you were suffering were so terrible, the children were very sick. There were no conditions.

But, also, that if you revealed that you were sick in any way, you would be taken away. And many people who were ill, understood to be ill, were taken away and never seen again and it was assumed that they were killed. You talk about how at times you did pray that you would not survive this, that you just could not take any more. And I did want to ask, how did you find the strength?

Ms. MAPENDO: The strength, I believe, is the strength from God, because first of all, I grew up in a

Christian house, but I was rejected that, like, resentful, according for what I have been through, but it was a pregnancy situation. Because in my belly, it was - the skin was coming off because sleep on the cement. The lice were everywhere.

And of course I still hungry. Like, when you feel hungry, when the baby's inside, you feel like baby is look like he wants to jump - to pass through your mouth. And I became weak and my body changed to yellow. And when I stood and I would feel dizzy, and I fell sometimes, down. And I thought my life was really freezing, stopped, and I thought I cannot pass. And I said, no matter what, there is a God - creation.

I came from somewhere and that God always give people choice. I believe in a God who put them in that situation. God can use people. And I made a decision to forgive the people who thought I am their enemy. And when I changed that, when I made the decision to forgive them, I became free from angry.

MARTIN: You made the truly remarkable, what many people consider the truly remarkable decision, to name your newborn twins after two of the prison guards.

Ms. MAPENDO: Yes.

MARTIN: Why did you do that?

Ms. MAPENDO: When you name somebody mean you love the person. But the decision to name the commanders who killed my husband, it was the way I try to think I can save my children's' life. And that way to try to tell them I am not your enemy. I know nobody understood, but

I do that because I forgive you no matter what. I am one of your people.

MARTIN: One of the most difficult things, I think, for any parent, though, is to see a child suffer. And your son, John, was beaten every day that you were in the camps. And your daughter, Amy, essentially saved his life. And what happened is that you made the decision to essentially give Amy to a soldier for a sex partner.

Ms. MAPENDO: Yes.

MARTIN: And I'd like to ask you if she has forgiven you.

Ms. MAPENDO: Yes. My daughter - I didn't - first of all, I love my daughter. I did - she knew I did not do because I hate her. She understood exactly the situation. And this is not - sometimes I think this is not our shame. It is not my shame either. It's not my daughter's either. It is the government's shame. I love my children. This is not my shame. And my daughter, I believe my daughter, she's forgiven. And we talked. I told my daughter before, I said, my mom, I will not leave you behind, because even though my daughter, she survived, but she pay a lot price. And I believe one day she's going to tell her own story -it will be in the public.

MARTIN: Well, as I said, it is a remarkable story and we do appreciate you being willing to talk about these very difficult things. As we are speaking now, there are many parts of the world which are in conflict, as you know. In the Ivory Coast is in the midst of a terrible, you know, political conflict, which has already led to the loss of life. There are a number of places around the world which are in conflict.

What do you feel - what do you think we can draw from your story?

Ms. MAPENDO: I believe it's everybody's responsibility to take the action to save these people's life. There are many thousands of people who are seeking for life, who need my help, who need my voice, who need your voice, who need the world's attention to save their life. If I forgive somebody, if I united by myself with somebody who kill my last husband, or somebody who tortured my life, somebody who kill my own people, you can try the best to unite with that person.

It's not to change the past, it's to change the future for your family, for your neighbor, for your friend. That's change your family. You know, be better, let our children pursue the happiness like everybody because the past is gone."

It is stories like these that need to be told regardless of how uncomfortable it might make the reader feel. Otherwise, to remain ignorant, and be in a constant state of denial, is to allow this colossal inhumanity to continue. There is, in fact, a powerful women's movement arising in all of Africa, and it needs the world's encouragement and continued support.

Elouise P Cobell

Eloise Pepion Cobell (1945 – 2011) was a Native American tribal elder in the Niitsitapi Blackfoot Confederacy. She was also known as the Yellow Bird Woman. In addition to her prestigious role in the tribe, she led an active and engaging life as a banker and rancher.

The Niisitapi (Blackfoot) people lived in the Northern Plains that occupied territory in the region that is now parts of Canada and the United States. Their history in the region is a long and involved (see images below).

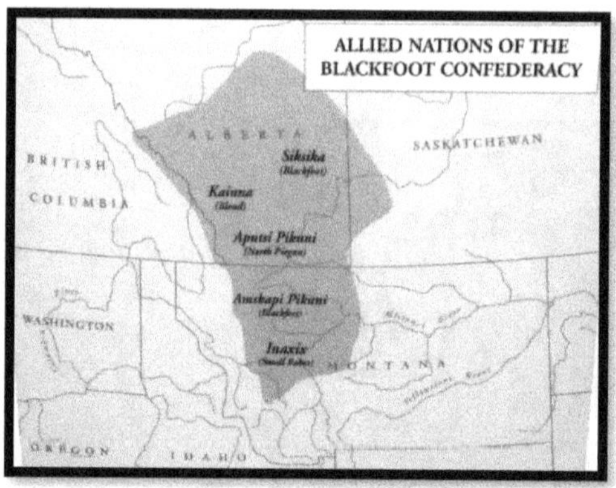

The Blackfoot Confederacy represents a conglomerate of four so-called, "First Nations" - Siksika (Northern Blackfoot), Kainah (Blood), South Pikuni (Piegan, located in Montana), and North Pikuni (Peigan, located in Alberta). All of these nations share a common language and heritage. Traditionally, they had a way of life centered around buffalo hunting.

The South Pikuni reside in Montana and the North Pikuni reside in Alberta, Canada. Tragically, there was a fifth group called the Small Robes that is no longer extant – the members of this group were wiped out by the smallpox epidemic of the 1830s.

The Blackfoot culture was rich in spirituality. According to the elders of the tribe (http://nativeamericannetroots.net/diary/1379) -

"Plains Indian culture was steeped in religion and ceremony. The world was an uncertain place, and people needed the help of supernatural powers.

"Help was obtained from the spirit world in the form of visions and dreams. In these dreams people were instructed in the use of sacred objects, songs, and rituals. These objects and rituals became part of the sacred Medicine Bundles.

"Medicine Bundles were the most powerful religious possession in Plains Indian culture. They were owned by individuals but could bring power, luck, or health to anyone who honoured them. Ownership of a bundle brought long life, success and social prestige."

Cobell was born on the Blackfoot Reservation in Montana. She had eight siblings and was the middle child. Her great grandmother was Mountain Chief - one of the esteemed leaders of the Blackfoot Nation. She grew up on her family's cattle ranch in harsh conditions without the benefit of electricity or running water.

In spite of the poverty of her upbringing, she attended Montana State University but had to curtail her education to care for her dying mother. Following her mother's passing, she moved to Seattle where she met and married Alvin Cobell a kinsman. They had one son, Turk Cobell. Ultimately, she returned to the reservation to assist with the management of the family ranch. She soon became treasurer for the Blackfoot Nation.

Cobell founded the Blackfeet National Bank – the first such bank on an Indian reservation. For her efforts and remarkable accomplishment, she won a McArthur genius award. Ultimately, twenty other tribes joined the bank to form the Native American Bank. Cobell became the Executive Director of a non-profit called, the "Native American Community Development Corporation."

On account her business and bookkeeping acumen, in 1996 Cobell was the lead plaintiff in a lawsuit against the federal government that challenged the country's mismanagement of the trust fund that involved half a million Native Americans. She pursued this suit that effectively demanded the government account for its distribution of fees from Indian-held resource leases. This class-action suit was referred to as, "Cobell v. Salazar."

This suit stems from the General Allotment Act of 1887 mandating that Indian reservations be divided into parcels for individual rather than collective ownership. The government than determined that many allottees were not capable of managing their own lands. As a consequence, the Department of the Interior (DOI) held these lands in trust, resulting in leasing the allotments for agricultural or mining activities. The revenues from these leases and royalties were supposed to the placed into individual Indian money accounts (IIMs) by the Bureau of Indian Affairs (BIA) to be paid to individual landowners. It is the management of this distribution that was effectively challenged in the suit.

Ultimately, the suit was successful, and a settlement was reached with the government. In response to the details of this settlement, Cobell said that, ""Although we have reached a settlement totaling more than $3.4 billion, there is little doubt this is significantly less than the full accounting to which individual Indians are entitled. Yes, we could prolong our struggle and fight longer, and perhaps one day we would know, down to the penny, how much individual Indians are owed. Perhaps we could even litigate long enough to increase the settlement amount. But we are compelled to settle now by the sobering realization that our class grows smaller each year, each month, and every day, as our elders die and are forever prevented from receiving their just compensation."

Without Cobell's unrelenting determination to right a grievous wrong done to her people, the injustice may have never been recognized and finally corrected.

Oscar Arias Sanchez

Oscar Arias Sanchez, born September 13, 1940 in Costa Rica was the winner of the Nobel Peace Prize in 1987. He studied law and economics at the University of Costa Rica in the nation's capital, San Jose. During his studies, he became involved in politics and joined the National Labor Party. On completion of this degree, he completed his post-graduate work in the United Kingdom (UK) with a doctorate – his graduate thesis was entitled, *Who Rules Costa Rica*. He was also a recipient of the Albert Schweitzer Prize for Humanitarianism and a trustee of Economists for Peace and Security. In addition, he also was also the author of a number of books including, *The Significance of the Student Movement in Costa Rica*.

During the 1970's he joined the Social Democratic Party and entered into public office in that era. He ultimately was elected to the presidency in 1986 when political torment and disorder plagued the region of Central American including a deadly civil war that was raging in Nicaragua – a situation that was further exacerbated by the involvement of the United States seeking to maintain its global hegemony and political and economic dominance in that region.

Sanchez sought to find a peaceful resolution to the turmoil that plagued Central America. As a consequence of his efforts, he designed a plan in 1978 that was ultimately approved by the governments of El Salvador, Honduras and Nicaragua. The goal of the strategy outlined in the plan was the implementation of free and fair elections, appropriate and verifiable safeguards for human rights and an end to foreign interference in the signatory countries internal affairs – this latter aspect of the agreement was particularly aimed at the United States government. In the process of formulating this agreement, Sanchez pushed back at the American government's attempt to alter the peace plan that was signed in 1987. He also refused to grant permission to allow the United States to use Costa Rican territory to provide logistical support to the Contras.

The following is Oscar Arias Sánchez's Acceptance Speech, on the occasion of the award of the Nobel Peace Prize in Oslo, December 10, 1987

"When you decided to honour me with this prize, you decided to honour a country of peace, you decided to honour Costa Rica. When in this year, 1987, you carried out the will of Alfred E. Nobel to encourage peace efforts in the world, you decided to encourage the efforts to secure peace in Central America. I am grateful for the recognition of our search for peace. We are all grateful in Central America.

"Nobody knows better than the honourable members of this Committee, that this prize is a sign to let the world know that you want to foster the Central American peace initiative. With your decision you are enhancing the possibilities of success. You are declaring how well you know the search for peace can never end, and how it is a permanent cause, always in need of true support from real friends, from people with courage to promote change in favour of peace, even against all odds.

"Peace is not a matter of prizes or trophies. It is not the product of a victory or command. It has no finishing line, no final deadline, no fixed definition of achievement.

"Peace is a never-ending process, the work of many decisions by many people in many countries. It is an attitude, a way of life, a way of solving problems and resolving conflicts. It cannot be forced on the smallest nation or enforced by the largest. It cannot ignore our differences or overlook our common interests. It requires us to work and live together.

"Peace is not only a matter of noble words and Nobel lectures. We have ample words, glorious words, inscribed in the charters of the United Nations, the World Court, the Organization of American States and a network of international treaties and laws. We need deeds that will respect those words, honour those commitments, abide by those laws. We need to strengthen our institutions of peace like the United Nations, making certain they are fully used by the weak as well as the strong.

"I pay no attention to those doubters and detractors unwilling to believe that a lasting peace can be genuinely embraced by those who march under a different ideological banner or those who are more accustomed to cannons of war than to councils of peace.

"We seek in Central America not peace alone, not peace to be followed someday by political progress, but peace and democracy, together, indivisible, an end to the shedding of human blood, which is inseparable from an end to the suppression of human rights. We do not judge, much less condemn, any other nation's political or ideological system, freely chosen and never exported. We cannot require sovereign states to conform to patterns of government not of their own choosing. But we can and do insist that every government respect those universal rights of man that have meaning beyond national boundaries and ideological labels. We believe that justice and peace can only thrive together, never apart. A nation that mistreats its own citizens is more likely to mistreat its neighbors.

"To receive this Nobel prize on the 10th of December is for me a marvelous coincidence. My son Oscar Felipe, here present, is eight years old today. I say to him, and through him to all the children of my country, that we shall never resort to violence, we shall never support military solutions to the problems of Central America. It is for the new generation that we must understand more than ever that peace can only be achieved through its own instruments: dialogue and understanding; tolerance and forgiveness; freedom and democracy.

"I know well you share what we say to all members of the international community, and particularly to those in the East and the West, with far greater power and resources than my small nation could never hope to possess, I say to them, with the utmost urgency: let Central Americans decide the future of Central America. Leave the interpretation and implementation of our peace plan to us. Support the efforts for peace instead of the forces of war in our region. Send our people ploughshares instead of swords, pruning hooks instead of spears. If they, for their own purposes, cannot refrain from amassing the weapons of war, then, in the name of God, at least they should leave us in peace.

"I say here to His Majesty and to the honourable members of the Nobel Peace Committee, to the wonderful people of Norway, that I accept this prize because I know how passionately you share our quest for peace, our eagerness for success. If, in the years to come peace prevails, and violence and war are thus avoided; a large part of that peace will be due to the faith of the people of Norway and will be theirs forever."

Oscar Arias Sanchez's unrelenting effort to create a social and political environment where peace and stability could be attained not only in Costa Rica but also throughout Central America remains to this day a model for others to emulate.

Denis Mukwege Mukengere

Dr. Denis Mukwege Mukengere from the Democratic Republic of the Congo (DRC) is currently the founder and medical director of Panzi Hospital in Bukavu – a commercial and industrial center of the country. He is the son of a Pentacostal pastor. Accompanying his father while he visited sick members of his community made a lasting impression on the young boy. This experience undoubtedly encouraged Mukengere to choose medicine as his profession; the Swedish Pentacostal mission provided support while he pursued this career. He decided upon gynecology and obstetrics as his specialties noting that female patients at Lemera Hospital did not have adequate medical care and, as a consequence, suffered unnecessary complications during their deliveries. He also realized that many of the women patients also suffered profoundly from the effects of sexually-induced violence.

He founded Panzi Hospital in 1999 specializing as a clinic for gynecological and obstetric care. Since the hospital's inception, Dr. Mukwege and his staff have helped to care for more than 50,000 survivors of sexual trauma. In addition to providing the necessary medical care, the hospital also provides legal, and psycho-social services to its patients. No patient is ever turned away for lack of sufficient financial resources.

Dr. Mukwege has been fearless in his efforts to increase protections for women and to insist that those responsible for sexual violence be brought to justice, including members of the Congolese government and militia groups laying siege to eastern DRC.

In October 2012, Dr. Mukwege was violently attacked, and his family was held at gunpoint at his home in an assassination attempt. Joseph Bizimana, his trusted friend and security guard, was killed. The attack came several weeks after Dr. Mukwege denounced the country's 16-year-long conflict and called for those responsible to be brought to justice during a speech at the United Nations. After this attack, Dr. Mukwege and his family fled the country for his safety, but his many Congolese patients and colleagues urged him to resume his life-saving work at Panzi Hospital. He returned to the hospital in January 2013 and was celebrated by crowds of people ecstatic to have him home. During this difficult period, Physicians for Human Rights (PHR) worked in close coordination with Dr. Mukwege and colleagues at risk in DRC to mobilize a global campaign to advocate for and protect individuals working on the front lines helping survivors of mass atrocities and prosecuting perpetrators of these horrific crimes against humanity.

Dr. Mukwege is also on the advisory committee for the International Campaign to Stop Rape and Gender Violence in Conflict. He has been the recipient of numerous awards worldwide, including the 2018 Nobel Peace Prize, for his advocacy against sexual violence as a weapon of war and for his outstanding services to survivors of rape.

The following is the full text of Mukengere's Nobel Prize acceptance speech awarded on December 10, 2018

"In the tragic night of 6 October 1996, rebels attacked our hospital in Lemera, in the Democratic Republic of Congo (RDC). More than thirty people were killed. Patients were slaughtered in their beds point blank. Unable to flee, the staff were killed in cold blood. I could not have imagined that it was only the beginning. Forced to leave Lemera in 1999, we set up the Panzi hospital in Bukavu where I still work as an obstetrician-gynecologist today.
The first patient admitted was a rape victim who had been shot in her genitals. The macabre violence knew no limit. Sadly, this violence has never stopped.

"One day like any other, the hospital received a phone call.

"At the other end of the line, a colleague in tears implored: "Please send us an ambulance fast. Please hurry."

"So, we sent an ambulance, as we normally do. Two hours later, the ambulance returned.

"Inside was a little girl about eighteen months old. She was bleeding profusely and was immediately taken to the operating room. When I arrived, all the nurses were sobbing. The baby's bladder, genitals and rectum were severely injured. By the penetration of an adult. We prayed in silence: my God, tell us what we are seeing isn't true. Tell us it's a bad dream. Tell us when we wake up, everything will be alright. But it was not a bad dream. It was the reality. It has become our new reality in the DRC.

"When another baby arrived, I realized that the problem could not be solved in the operating room, but that we had to combat the root causes of these atrocities. I decided to travel to the village of Kavumu to talk to the men: why don't you protect your babies, your daughters, your wives? And where are the authorities? To my surprise, the villagers knew the suspect. Everyone was afraid of him, since he was a member of the provincial Parliament and enjoyed absolute power over the population. For several months, his militia has been terrorizing the whole village. It had instilled fear by killing a human rights defender who had had the courage to report the facts. The deputy got away with no consequences. His parliamentary immunity enabled him to abuse with impunity.

"The two babies were followed by several dozens of other raped children. When the forty-eighth victim arrived, we were desperate. With other human rights defenders, we went to a military court. At last, the rapes were prosecuted and judged as crimes against humanity. The rapes of babies in Kavumu stopped. And so did the calls to Panzi hospital. But these babies' psychological, sexual and reproductive health is severely impaired.

"What happened in Kavumu and what is still going on in many other places in Congo, such as the rapes and massacres in Béni and Kasaï, was made possible by the absence of the rule of law, the collapse of traditional values and the reign of impunity, particularly for those in power. Rape, massacres, torture, widespread insecurity and a flagrant lack of education create a spiral of unprecedented violence.

"The human cost of this perverted, organized chaos has been hundreds of thousands of women raped, over 4 million people displaced within the country and the loss of 6 million human lives. Imagine, the equivalent of the entire population of Denmark decimated.

"United Nations peacekeepers and experts have not been spared, either. Several of them have been killed on duty. Today, the United Nations Mission is still in the DRC to prevent the situation from degenerating further. We are grateful to them.

"However, despite their efforts, this human tragedy will continue if those responsible are not prosecuted. Only the fight against impunity can break the spiral of violence.

We all have the power to change the course of history when the beliefs we are fighting for are right.

"Your Majesties, Your Royal Highnesses, Your Excellencies, Distinguished members of the Nobel Committee, dear Madam Nadia Murad, Ladies and Gentlemen, Friends of peace, It is in the name of the Congolese people that I accept the Nobel Peace Prize. It is to all victims of sexual violence across the world that I dedicate this prize. It is with humility that I come before you to raise the voice of the victims of sexual violence in armed conflicts and the hopes of my compatriots. I take this opportunity to thank everyone who, over the years, has supported our battle. I am thinking, in particular, of the organizations and institutions of friendly countries, my colleagues, my family and my dear wife Madeleine.

"My name is Denis Mukwege. I come from one of the richest countries on the planet. Yet the people of my country are among the poorest of the world. The troubling reality is that the abundance of our natural resources – gold, coltan (a dull black metallic ore from which the elements niobium and tantalum are extracted), cobalt and other strategic minerals – is the root cause of war, extreme violence, and abject poverty. We love nice cars, jewelry, and gadgets. I have a smartphone myself. These items contain minerals found in our country. Often mined in inhuman conditions by young children, victims of intimidation and sexual violence. When you drive your electric car; when you use your smart phone or admire your jewelry, take a minute to reflect on the human cost of manufacturing these objects. As consumers, let us at least insist that these products are manufactured with respect for human dignity. Turning a blind eye to this tragedy is being complicit. It's not just perpetrators of violence who are responsible for their crimes, it is also those who choose to look the other way.

"My country is being systematically looted with the complicity of people claiming to be our leaders. Looted for their power, their wealth, and their glory. Looted at the expense of millions of innocent men, women and children abandoned in extreme poverty. While the profits from our minerals end up in the pockets of a predatory oligarchy.

"For twenty years now, day after day, at Panzi hospital, I have seen the harrowing consequences of the country's gross mismanagement. Babies, girls, young women, mothers, grandmothers, and also men and boys, cruelly raped, often publicly and collectively, by inserting burning plastic or sharp objects in their genitals. I'll spare you the details. The Congolese people have been humiliated, abused and massacred for more than two decades in plain sight of the international community. Today, with access to the most powerful communication technology ever, no one can say: "I didn't know."

"With this Nobel Peace Prize, I call on the world to be a witness and I urge you to join us in order to put an end to this suffering that shames our common humanity.

The people of my country desperately need peace.

But:

How to build peace on mass graves?

"How to build peace without truth nor reconciliation?

"How to build peace without justice nor reparation?

"As I speak to you, a report is gathering mold in an office drawer in New York. It was drafted following a professional investigation into war crimes and human rights violations perpetrated in Congo. This investigation explicitly names the victims, the places and the dates, but leaves the perpetrators nameless.

"This Mapping Report by the office of the United Nations High Commissioner for Human Rights describes no fewer than 617 war crimes and crimes against humanity and perhaps even crimes of genocide.

"What is the world waiting for before taking this into account? There is no lasting peace without justice. Yet, justice in not negotiable. Let us have the courage to take a critical and impartial look at what has been going on for too long in the Great Lakes Region. Let us have the courage to reveal the names of the perpetrators of the crimes against humanity to prevent them from continuing to plague the region. Let us have the courage to recognize our past mistakes. Let us have the courage to tell the truth, to remember and commemorate. Dear Congolese compatriots let us have the courage to take our destiny in our own hands. Let us build peace, build our country's future, and together build a better future for Africa. No one else will do it for us.

"Ladies and Gentlemen, Friends of peace, The picture I have painted for you depicts a dark reality.

"But let me tell you Sarah's story. Sarah was referred to the hospital in critical condition. An armed group had attacked her village, massacred her whole family, and had left her alone. Sarah was taken to the forest as a hostage and tied to a tree. Naked. Sarah was gang-raped every day until she lost consciousness.

"The aim of these rapes used as a weapon of war is to destroy the victim, her family and her community. In short, to destroy the social fabric. When she arrived at the hospital, Sarah could not walk or even stand on her feet. She could not control her bladder nor her bowels. Because of the seriousness of her genital, urinary and digestive injuries coupled with an infection, no one could imagine her one day being able to get back on her feet. Yet, with each passing day, the desire to continue to live sparkled in Sarah's eyes. Every passing day, it was she who encouraged the medical staff not to lose hope. Today, Sarah is a beautiful, smiling, strong and charming woman. Sarah has committed herself to helping people who have survived a history like hers.

Sarah received fifty US dollars, a grant our Dorcas transit house gives to women who are ready to rebuild their lives socio-economically.

"Today, Sarah runs her small business. She has bought a plot of land. The Panzi Foundation has helped her with sheeting to make a roof. She has built a little house. She is independent and proud.

"Her experience shows that, no matter how difficult and hopeless the situation, with determination there is always hope at the end of the tunnel. If a woman like Sarah does not give up, who are we to do so? This is Sarah's story. Sarah is Congolese. But there are Sarahs in the Central African Republic, Colombia, Bosnia, Myanmar, Iraq and many other conflict-riven countries in the world.

"At Panzi, our holistic care programme – which includes medical, psychological, socio-economic, and legal support – shows that even if the road to recovery is long and difficult, victims have the potential to turn their suffering into power. They can become agents of positive change in society. This is the case already at City of Joy, our rehabilitation centre in Bukavu where women receive support to regain control of their destiny. However, they cannot succeed on their own and our role is to listen to them, as today we listen to Madam Nadia Murad. Dear Nadia, your courage, your audacity, your ability to give us hope, are a source of inspiration for the entire world and for me personally.

"The Nobel Peace Prize awarded to us today will be of value only if it leads to concrete change in the lives of victims of sexual violence all over the world and the restoration of peace in our countries. So, what can we do? What can you do? First, it is incumbent upon all of us to act in this direction. Taking action is a choice. It is a choice:

– whether or not we stop violence against women,

– whether or not we create a positive masculinity which promotes gender equality, in times of peace and in times of war.

"It is a choice:

- whether or not to support a woman,

– whether or not to protect her,

– whether or not to defend her rights,

– whether or not to fight on her side in countries ravaged by conflict.

"It is a choice: whether or not to build peace in the countries in conflict.

"Taking action means saying 'no' to indifference.

"If there is a war to be waged, it is the war against the indifference which is eating away at our societies. Second, we are all indebted to these women and their loved-ones and we must all take ownership of this fight; including states by ceasing to welcome leaders who have tolerated, or worse, used sexual violence to take power. States must stop welcoming them by rolling out the red carpet, and instead draw a red line against the use of rape as a weapon of war. This red line would consist of imposing economic and political sanctions on these leaders and taking them to court. Doing the right thing is not hard. It is a matter of political will. Third, we must acknowledge the suffering of the survivors of all acts of violence against women in armed conflicts and support their holistic recovery process.

"I insist on reparations: the measures that give survivors compensation and satisfaction and enable them to start a new life. It is a human right. I call on States to support the initiative to create a Global Fund for reparations for victims of sexual violence in armed conflicts. Fourth, on behalf of all widows, all widowers and orphans of the massacres committed in the DRC and all Congolese in love with peace, I call on the international community to finally consider the "Mapping Project report" and its recommendations. May justice prevail.

"This would allow the Congolese people to weep for their loved-ones, to mourn their dead, to forgive their torturers, to overcome their suffering and finally to project themselves into a serene future. Finally, after twenty years of bloodshed, rape and massive population displacements, the Congolese people are desperately awaiting implementation of the responsibility to protect the civilian population when their government cannot or does not want to do so. The people are waiting to explore the path to a lasting peace. To achieve peace, there has to be adherence to the principle of free, transparent, credible and peaceful elections.

"People of the Congo, let us get to work!" Let's build a State at the heart of Africa where the government serves its people. A State under the rule of law, capable of bringing lasting and harmonious development not just of the DRC but of the whole of Africa, where all political, economic and social actions will be based on a people-centered approach to restore human dignity of all citizens.

"Your Majesties, Distinguished Members of the Nobel Committee, Ladies and Gentlemen, Friends of peace, The challenge is clear. It is within our reach. For all Sarah's, for all women, for all men and children of Congo, I call upon you not only to award this Nobel Peace Prize to my country's people, but to stand up and together say loudly: The violence in the DRC, it's enough! Enough is enough! Peace, now!

Thank you."

The story of Dr. Mukengere's response to the human atrocities he witnessed as a caring and compassionate physician is one of remarkable tenacity and courage in the face of formidable odds at considerable risk to his own personal safety and that of his associates, friends, and family. The message he conveyed in the body of his Nobel Peace Prize acceptance speech to his distinguished audience was filled with remarkable moral clarity, integrity, and indefatigable courage and conviction.

Maxima Acuna De Chapeu

Over the recent past, Peru has experienced accelerated growth in the mining industry. With the prospect of increasing employment and the possibility of much-needed revenues coming from resource development as promised by competing mining interests, the government of Peru has awarded mining licenses throughout the country, especially in the Northern Peruvian Highlands of Cajamarca where it has been estimated that nearly one-half of the land in this region has been consigned to mining interests. In the regions impacted by this growth in mining, the rural campesinos effected remain in poverty and have felt the deleterious environmental impact that is an inevitable consequence of mining operations, especially heavy-metal water pollution that has profound consequences to both health and agriculture.

For example, Colorado-based Newmont and Buenaventura, a Peruvian mining company, jointly own and operate the Yanacocha Mine – a highly profitable gold and copper mining operation. As this operation was becoming exhausted of these precious materials, its owners looked elsewhere and in 2010 proposed the development of a new site for the mining of gold, the Conga Mine, ten miles from Yanacocha. This project involved draining four nearby lakes and transforming one of these lakes, Laguna Azul into an initial mining site. This project would ultimately threaten the headwaters of five significant watersheds in the Cajamarca Paramo ecosystem, a high-altitude wetland.

Máxima Acuña's personal story is indicative of the plight of native peoples in Peru and elsewhere in South America. Acuña and her husband purchased land in a rural section of Peru's northern highlands – Tragadero Grande. They built a small house and managed a modest farm growing potatoes and other crops as well as managing sheep and cows for the production of cheese and milk. There, they raised a family and felt safe and secure within their apparently peaceful environment. What they did not realize was the fact that Newmont and Buenaventura Mining sought to incorporate her land to fulfill their goal of developing the Conga mine.

The harassment and cruelty that Acuña had to endure at the hands of the mining company in collusion with the Peruvian government was quite extraordinary. The mining company demanded that the family had to abandon their home. When Acuña refused, armed forces came, destroyed the family's home and possessions, and physically abused her and one of her daughters. In addition, the mining company brought the family to court and sued for squatting on their own land. At the end of this legal battle, Acuña was found guilty and fined nearly $2000 dollars – a remarkable sum for a subsistence farmer.

Undeterred and determined to resist this assault on her and her family's rights, Acuña sought help from GRUFIDES (http://grufides.org) – a non-governmental organization (NGO,) created to advocate for the native peoples of Cajamarca (see map below) in response to the incursion of mining interests in the region.

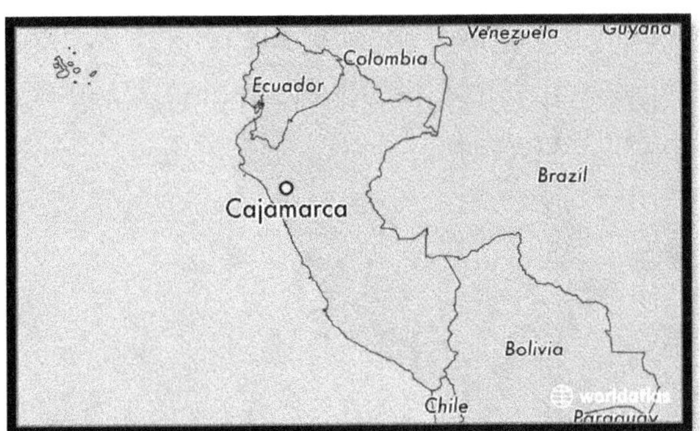

With the assistance of her attorney, Mirtha Vasquez, Acuña appealed the court ruling against her using official documents that showed that she held legitimate title to the land erroneously claimed by the mining company. Finally, in December 2014, the court found in her favor. As a result, the Conga mine failed to expand into Tragadero Grande.

In spite of this apparent legal victory, Acuña was still subjected to relentless harassment on the part of the mining company and its paid security contractors. For example, a fence was built around her land, her potato crops were willfully destroyed, and she and her family were placed under intense scrutiny with the aim of preventing Acuña from planting additional crops in the hopes of ultimately driving them off the property. Currently, the legal battles continue in the Peruvian Supreme Court.

Regardless of this horrific assault on her way of life, her livelihood, and her well-being, Acuña has maintained her indomitable determination and optimism. As a result, she continues to be an inspiration for those who are suffering daily from the impact of the relentless harassment and intimidation perpetrated by mining interests in the region and elsewhere.

Cecile Ann Hansen

Cecile Ann Hansen - a descendant of Chief Si'ahl (Chief Seattle – 1786-1866) - has been the elect chair of the Duwamish people since 1975. Hansen's goal since her rise to this position has been to correct injustices perpetrated against her people. These injustices include:

•Loss of traditional tribal lands – Seattle and much of present-day King County as a result of the Point Elliot Treaty of 1855

•Loss of fishing rights along the Duwamish River

•Refusal of the federal government to grant the tribe recognition as a legitimate historic tribe.

When the first European-American settlers arrived in the Pacific Northwest, it was the Duwamish and Suquamish people who embraced the newcomers and helped them in their efforts to thrive in the region. Chief Si' ahl held his position as head of the tribe for twenty-six years until his death in 1866.

Cecile Hansen whose parents are Charles H. Oliver and Margaret K. Oliver (Holmes), the great-great-grand niece of Chief Si'ahl. As a young child, she moved frequently with her family – her father worked as a logger and a fisherman. She lived for a time at Taholah, Pacific Beach, Seattle's Holly Park housing projects, Aberdeen, Grayland, Tokeland, South Bend and Burien Washington where she attended Highline High School and graduated in 1955.

She met a serviceman, Charles Williams, a member of the Quileute tribe; they were married in 1955 and moved to the reservation in Queets where they had several children. During her time on the reservation, she was distressed by the living conditions she witnessed all around her. This would leave a lasting impression and helped determine the path her life would eventually take. Her third husband, Howard Hansen died in 1999.

The Duwamish tribe was guaranteed fishing rights as specifically cited in the 1855 Point Elliot Treaty – and yet was systematically denied those rights by the state of Washington. The following are sections of that treaty that are pertinent to this discussion – special attention should be placed on Article 5. It should also be noted that Duwamish tribe is clearly listed as one of the signatories to that treaty (a partial listing shown below) of which there were many. On examination of this treaty, it becomes quite apparent that it clearly represents a taking of Native American-occupied territory with little benefit accruing to the signatories. It was the complete abrogation of the treaty regarding native fishing rights that triggered the so-called Fish Wars in the 1960s.

The Treaty of Point Elliot – January 22, 1855 (President James Buchanan)

Article 4

"The said tribes and bands agree to remove to and settle upon the said first above-mentioned reservations within one year after the ratification of this treaty, or sooner, if the means are furnished them. In the meantime it shall be lawful for them to reside upon any land not in the actual claim and occupation of citizens of the United States, and upon any land claimed or occupied, if with the pemission of the owner."

Article 5

"The right of taking fish at usual and accustomed grounds and stations is further secured to said Indians in common with all citizens of the Territory, and of erecting temporary houses for the purpose of curing, together with the privilege of hunting and gathering roots and berries on open and unclaimed lands. Provided, however, That they shall not take shell-fish from any beds staked or cultivated by citizens."

Joseph Aprile   Cecile Ann Hansen

Article 6

"In consideration of the above cession, the United States agree to pay to the said tribes and bands the sum of one hundred and fifty thousand dollars, in the following manner - - that is to say: For the first year after the ratification hereof, fifteen thousand dollars; for the next two years, twelve thousand dollars each year; for the next three years, ten thousand dollars each year; for the next four years, seven thousand five hundred dollars each year; for the next five years, six thousand dollars each year; and for the last five years, four thousand two hundred and fifty dollars each year. All which said sums of money shall be applied to the use and benefit of the said Indians, under the direction of the President of the United States, who may, from time to time, determine at his discretion upon what beneficial objects to expend the same; and the superintendent of Indian affairs, or other proper officer, shall each year inform the President of the wishes of said Indians in respect thereto."

<u>Signatories</u>

Issac I. Stevens, Governor and Superintendent. (L.S.)

Seattle, Chief of the Duwamish and Suquamish tribes, his x mark. (L. S.)

Pat-ka-nam, Chief of the Snoqualmoo, Snohomish and other tribes, his x mark. (L.S.)

Chow-its-hoot, Chief of the Lummi and other tribes, his x mark. (L. S.)

Goliah, Chief of the Skagits and other allied tribes, his x mark. (L.S.)

Kwallattum, or General Pierce, Sub-chief of the Skagit tribe, his x mark. (L.S.)

S'hootst-hoot, Sub-chief of Snohomish, his x mark. (L.S.)

Once Hansen was elected chair, she conducted a survey of tribal members to determine what their most urgent concerns were. As a result of this survey, she found that her people wanted recognition by the federal government as to their unique and continual existence as a unique Native American culture and, most importantly, of their land base. With this information in hand, an appeal was drafted to the U.S. government that outlined this desire to be recognized as an intact and viable Indian Nation in 1977. This would prove to be the beginning of an exceedingly prolonged process.

As a result of an on-going dispute regarding Indian fishing rights, a case was heard in the United States District Court for the Western District of Washington State – *United States v. Washington*. Federal Judge George Boldt's ruling did affirm that treaty rights permitted the continued harvesting of salmon. However, it was also determined that, "at all usual and accustomed grounds and stations" (as typical treaties stated), the Duwamish -- as a tribe not yet recognized by the government -- were (along with the Samish, Snohomish, Snoqualmie, and Steilacoom peoples) excluded."

Although Hansen first started the process of trying to achieve federal legal recognition of the Duwamish Tribe, in 1977, that dream remains unfulfilled. Nearing the end of President Bill Clinton's administration, that recognition was briefly granted by the Bureau of Indian Affairs (BIA). But this recognition was short-lived; for, the decision was subsequently overturned by the BIA under the aegis of the administration of President George W. Bush.

In spite of this drawback, Hansen persists in her efforts to this day. She has proven herself to be an unflinching advocate for her people.

Pramila Jayapal

Pramila Jayapal is a member of the U.S. House of Representatives representing Washington's 7th Congressional District. Jayapal began her career in the U.S. Congress in 2016 when she won 56 percent of votes to defeat fellow Democrat Brady Walkinshaw.

Jayapal was formerly Washington State Senator representing the state's 37th District. She is well known for her progressive views and has repeatedly spoken out passionately for an open and all-inclusive society that embraces the many diverse voices that constitute contemporary America.

Jayapal was born in Chennai India and grew up in Indonesia and Singapore. At the age of 16, she emigrated to the United States to further her education and earned her bachelor's degree from Georgetown University and a Master of Business Administration (MBA) from Northwestern University.

Her professional career began as a financial analyst working for PaineWebber — a well-established financial services company. Overtime, she began applying her skills to projects focusing on social services and ultimately became involved in the political process. The terrorist attacks on the World Trade Center in New York City on September 11, 2001 and the resulting burgeoning of hatred towards immigrant groups in the United States had such a profound impact on Jayapal that she founded the Hate Free Zone as way to provide support for the nation's immigrants. This organization has been involved in helping new American citizens to register to vote and serves as an advocacy group for immigration reform. Hate Free Zone successfully sued the Immigration and Naturalization Services during the administration of George W. Bush for its attempt to deport thousands of Somalis residing throughout the country. Jayapal resigned her leadership position in Hate Free Zone in 2012; however, this organization remains in existence (hatefreezone.org).

Jayapal's political career began when she served on Seattle's Mayor Advisory Committee where she was a strong advocate for raising the minimum wage to 15 dollars an hour that eventually became law. In 2014 she entered the political arena campaigning to fill a seat in the Washington State Senate and she went on to win that seat in November 2014. In her position as State Senator, she was a strong advocate for women's rights and for people of color.

In January of 2016 Jayapal announced her plans to run for United States Congress for a seat in the House of Representatives for the 7th congressional district in Washington state. She won that election with 56 percent of the vote. Since his inauguration as President, Trumps has repeatedly attempted to implement so-called "zero-tolerance" policies regarding immigration. His apparent disregard for the human suffering such an approach imparts upon the men, woman and families who are seeking a better life for themselves, inspired Jayapal to participate in the Women Disobey protest and sit-in at the Hart Senate Office building on June 28, 2018. She was subsequently arrested along with 500 others.

As an outspoken member of the House of Representatives and a staunch advocate of progressive legislation, Jayapal co-sponsored legislation that would make public colleges and universities tuition-free for a majority of families and reduce mounting student debt that is approaching crisis proportions throughout the country. She also has been involved in the United for Climate and Environmental Justice Task Force. In addition, she has co-sponsored the Expanded and Improved Medicare for All Act.

In addition to her efforts on domestic issues regarding social justice, Jayapal has also been active regarding global issues of peace and social justice.

Jayapal voted against a House resolution condemning the U.N. Security Council resolution on Israeli settlements built on the occupied Palestinian territories in the West Bank. In July 2019, Jayapal voted against H. Res.

246, a House resolution introduced by Congressman Brad Schneider (D-IL) opposing efforts to delegitimize the State of Israel and the Global Boycott, Divestment, and Sanctions Movement targeting Israel. The resolution passed 398-17.

On April 25, 2018, 57 members of the House of Representatives, including Jayapal released a condemnation of Holocaust distortion in Poland and Ukraine. They criticized Poland's new Holocaust law, which would criminalize accusing Poles of complicity in the Holocaust, and Ukraine's 2015 memory laws glorifying Ukrainian Insurgent Army (UPA) and its pro-Nazi leaders, such as Roman Shukhevych.

In April 2019, after the House passed the resolution withdrawing American support for the Saudi-led coalition in Yemen, Jayapal was one of nine lawmakers to sign a letter to President Trump requesting a meeting with him and urging him to put his signature to Senate Joint Resolution 7, which invokes the War Powers Act of 1973 to end unauthorized US military participation in the Saudi-led coalition's armed conflict against Yemen's Houthi forces, initiated in 2015 by the Obama administration. Within this resolution it was asserted that the "Saudi-led coalition's imposition of an air-land-and-sea blockade as part of its war against Yemen's Houthis has continued to prevent the unimpeded distribution of these vital commodities, contributing to the suffering and death of vast numbers of civilians throughout the country." The signatories of this letter felt that the President's approval of this resolution might apply appropriate pressure to the Saudi-led coalition to bring the four-year-old war to a close.

In June 2019, Jayapal became the first South Asian American woman to preside over the House.

Her duties and responsibilities in filling this position included:

- Senior Whip, Democratic Caucus of the United States House of Representatives
- Vice Ranking Member, United States House Committee on the Budget
- Co-chair, Congressional Progressive Caucus
- Co-chair and co-founder, United for Climate and Environmental Justice Task Force
- Chair, Immigration Task Force, Congressional Asian Pacific American Caucus (CAPAC)
- Co-chair, Women's Working Group on Immigration Reform
- DNC Transition Team Member.

The horrific terrorist attack of the World Trade Center in New York on September 11, 2001 made such a deep and lasting impression on Jayapal that she felt compelled to come to terms with the destabilizing influence that this event had upon the national psyche. As a result, she founded *OneAmerica* (initially called the Hate Free Zone as described earlier) and served as executive director of the organization for 11 years. OneAmerica describes its purpose as "organizing with and advocating for diverse communities" and was initially founded to "address the backlash, hate crimes, and discrimination against immigrant communities of color, primarily Muslims, Arab Americans, East Africans, and South Asians," according to its website.

Jayapal has repeatedly demonstrated her resolve to speak out on issues that address civil rights and equality no matter how apparently controversial. In keeping with this determined and unabashed support of equal rights, the Congresswoman has spoken out in support of the Lesbian, Gay, Bisexual and Transgender community (LGBTQ) even when it impacted her own child, Janak.

In this regard, Jayapal gave an emotional speech about her gender-nonconforming child while advocating for LGBTQ civil rights legislation, saying her child had discovered "newfound freedom".

She displayed deep emotions as she talked about the personal impact of her child embracing their gender identity. She expressed her feelings in the following way, "I didn't intend to say this today, but my beautiful now 22-year-old child told me last year that they were gender non-conforming, and over the last year, I have come to understand from a deeply personal mother's perspective … their newfound freedom … to rid themselves of some conformist stereotype of who they are, to be able to express who they are at their real core."

Jayapal, speaking at a House committee hearing, said her children had always done well in school but had carried a "heavy burden of conflict in their own being, that I could not fully identify or help to express." She went on to say that "the deeply impactful moment" of her child embracing their gender has allowed for "their creativity, their brilliance, their self-expression." Jayapal continued, "My children are free to be who they are, and in that freedom comes a responsibility for us as legislators to protect that freedom."

The moving speech in support of the Equality Act, that would provide non-discrimination protections for LGBTQ people across the country, was a rare moment of an elected representative speaking out about gender-nonconforming and non-binary identity, meaning people who identify themselves as neither male nor female.

Jayapal, who was a Seattle civil rights activist before she was elected, talked about her children at a time when LGBTQ rights, and trans rights in particular, are under attack in the U.S. In recent years, more people have come out as gender-fluid or non-binary. As a matter of fact, a recent study in Minnesota estimated that 3% of teenagers identify as trans or non-conforming.

Many U.S. states have recognized a third gender option, allowing people to identify as non-binary on their state IDs.

The Equality Act would establish consistent protections for LGBTQ people in employment, housing, credit, education, and other areas.

Given that queer and trans youth experience high rates of family rejection and violence, advocates pointed out that is was especially powerful to see a parent publicly celebrate their child.

Jayapal also drew attention to the fact that public spaces that are trans-inclusive, allowing people to access facilities that match their gender, do not threaten cisgender people.

"We're talking about fear versus love. We're talking about fear versus freedom," she said.

As an influential personality in public life, Jayapal has consistently demonstrated an unwavering advocacy for civil and individual rights for all people regardless of their ethnic, social, religious, cultural, and sexual affiliations. She has done so with remarkable courage, persistence, and determination.

Fred Korematsu

Given the current political and national climate in regard to immigration and the status of the foreign born, especially people of color, the story of Fred Korematsu, a Japanese American, is of special significance.

It has been over 75 years since Fred Korematsu was arrested on the suspicion that he was Japanese and therefore had not surrendered his personal freedom pursuant to Executive Order 9066 promulgated by the administration of President Franklin D Roosevelt (February 19, 1942). This executive order directed the immediate and enforced internment of Americans of Japanese descent. Pursuant to this order, 110,000 Japanese Americans were forcefully moved to concentration camps.

Joseph Aprile   Fred Korematsu

Fred Korematsu was walking down a street in San Leandro, California when police arrested him on Memorial Day 1942. Korematsu subsequently proclaimed that he refused to comply with this order. He was a welder by profession born in Oakland, California to Japanese-American parents.

Following his arrest, when questioned at police headquarters, Korematsu at first lied about his own personal identity claiming he was Clyde Sarah and of Spanish and Hawaiian ancestry. In fact, he carried with him an obviously altered draft card with false information. Eventually, he told the authorities the truth and that his family was living in what was euphemistically referred to as a "relocation camp."

After this admission, he was forcibly taken to the Tanforan Assembly Center – a former racetrack where 7800 individuals were being held along with his parents and three brothers. He was placed in what used to be a horse stall with few amenities. "These camps [are] definitely an imprisonment under armed guard with orders [to] shoot to kill," Korematsu wrote in a note to his lawyer. "These people should have been given a fair trial in order that they may defend their loyalty at court in a democratic way."

Over time, Korematsu became determined to challenge his fate in court having some confidence in the capacity of the court system to render a just verdict. During his trial in Federal Court in San Francisco, Korematsu speaking in his own defense said, "As a citizen of the United States I am ready, willing, and able to bear arms for this country." He went on to say that he had registered for the draft and attempted to volunteer his service in the U.S. Navy. He also said that he had never been to Japan and could not read Japanese. The judge in the case, nevertheless, found him guilty of disobeying the removal order and sentenced him to five years' probation and was ordered to be taken back to the internment camp.

Although his parents and family were not happy with his decision to defy the Executive Order and despite the general impression that the occupants of these internment camps remained docile, historic evidence gathered in the interim paints a very different picture. In fact, there were acts of civil disobedience and reported unrest on the part of the involuntary occupants in these camps.

Beginning in November of 1942, Korematsu was given leave to live and work outside the camp – this was a partial freedom granted to younger "detainees" of working age. Finally, in January 1944, near the end of the war, Korematsu was given indefinite leave from the camp.

During this time, Korematsu's lawyers brought his cast to the Federal Court of Appeals that ultimately upheld his original conviction finding that Executive Order 9066 was constitutional. Subsequently, his case came before the U.S. Supreme Court - Korematsu v. U.S. - in October of 1944 and on December 18, 1944 the court upheld the constitutionality of the Executive Order in a 6-3 decision claiming that at the time of the internment there was a "military urgency."

Three justices wrote minority dissents. Justice Robert H, Jackson wrote, "The Court for all time has validated the principle of racial discrimination in criminal procedure and of transplanting American citizens. The principle then lies about like a loaded weapon, ready for the hand of any authority that can bring forward a plausible claim of an urgent need."

After the war, when the Korematsu family returned to Oakland they found their flower nursery in a pitiful state having been neglected by the tenants. Thousands of detainees felt that on release they would have nowhere to go in safety; therefore, they decided to remain in the camps until they were ultimately closed in May 1946.

Korematsu subsequently married, had children, and finally moved back to California. In 1981, evidence was uncovered that the U.S. government had presented fallacious evidence to the Supreme Court in Korematsu's case and had effectively suppressed information as to the loyalty of Japanese American citizens to the U.S. Finally, his case was brought back to the federal court in 1983 and his conviction was thrown out.

Following this favorable decision that vindicated him, Korematsu became active in the arena of civil rights and civil liberties. He lobbied Congress to pass the Civil Liberties Act of 1988, that offered compensation and an apology to former wartime detainees. In 1998, he was awarded the Presidential Medal of Freedom by President Bill Clinton in recognition for his relentless valor and determination to act in defense of individual liberties as firmly established in the Constitution of the United States .

Before his death in 2005, he filed a court brief in support of the civil rights of Guantanamo Bay detainees that was brought before the U.S. Supreme Court. In 2010, in a tribute to his unflinching and courageous actions in support of basic civil liberties, California made his birthday, January 30, Fred Korematsu Day of Civil Liberties and the Constitution.

Gordon Hirabayashi

We have previously examined the life of Fred Korematsu, above, and have seen the degree of his courage in opposing the involuntary internment of Japanese-Americans during World War II. There was yet another individual, Gordon Hirabayashi, who openly defied Order No. 9066 that forcefully relocated so many Japanese-Americans, brutally uprooted them from their lives and livelihoods and for many their property as well.

Hirabayashi was born on April 23, 1918, in Sandpoint, Washington to Shungo and Mitsuko Hirabayashi who emigrated from Nagano Prefecture, Japan – a farming community. Shungo came to the United States in 1907 and was later to marry Mitsuko in 1914. It was an arranged marriage that was not uncommon in that era. Both Shungo and Mitsuko had studied at the Kenshi Gijuku Academy in Japan where they had learned English and eventually converted to the Christian religion. Rather than joining a conventional Christian mainline church they became followers of Kanzo Uchimura (1861 – 1930) who was responsible for founding the Mukyokai movement in Japan. The emphasis of this mode of Christianity proposed a non-liturgical approach to religious practice. It became known for its non-church services.

In 1891, Uchimura gained notoriety when, as a teacher at the First Higher School in Tokyo, he refused to bow before the signature of the emperor affixed to a copy of the new Imperial Rescript on Education. He later changed his mind and from a sickbed sent a colleague to bow for him, but the affair effectually ended his educational career. The Mukoyokai movement was pacifist in its orientation and stressed that behavior should reflect belief. It was apparently this ideology that inspired Hirabyashi to act in a way that lived up to his beliefs.

Once in America, Hirabayashi's parents were instrumental with others in forming the White River Garden Corporation. In order to accomplish this, the Japanese-American members had to use a white intermediary on account of the fact that the Washington State Constitution had incorporated an alien land law in its founding documents in 1889. In 1921, this law was amended to make it impossible for aliens ineligible for citizenship to hold major shares in a corporation, hold property or hold any major interest in lands delegated for agricultural use. Because of this legal stipulation, the White River Garden

Corporation lost its case in the Washington State Supreme Court and the farmland was ceded to the State, but the families involved were allowed to stay on the land and rent it from the State.

Given his unique Christian upbringing, he began to take a pacifist stance in regard to the growing conflict that was embracing Europe and Asia. By 1939 following the German occupation of Poland, the United Kingdom had declared war on Germany. As a consequence of these events, Hirabayashi as a young man registered with the Selective Service as a conscientious objector and joined the Religious Society of Friends, the Quakers, known for their long-standing pacifist theology.

Following the Japanese attack on Pearl Harbor on December 7, 1941, it was becoming quite evident that the United States domestic policy had begun to focus on Japanese-Americans as possible being a potential threat to domestic security. Finally, with the promulgation of Executive Order 9066, the military was given the responsibility of implementing the forced migration of Japanese-Americans living on the West Coast to hastily constructed internment camps.

Realizing that his constitutionally mandated rights were being violated, he made the momentous and courageous decision to resist. When the time came requiring him to register for relocation, Hirabayashi turned himself in to the Federal Bureau of Investigation (FBI). His strategy was to create a test case as a way to challenge the underlying constitutionality of the federal mandate that ordered the forced incarceration of an entire group without due process of law. He had an underlying faith in the democratic system. He received a substantial amount of legal help and was eventually represented by Frank L. Waters. He was also supported by the American Friends Service Committee and Norman Thomas (1884 – 1968), the noted pacifist and leader of the Socialist Party of the United States for many years.

On May 13, 942, Hirabayashi wrote the following letter (see the image below) –

Joseph Aprile
Gordon Hirabayashi

Why I refused to register for evacuation:

Over and above any man-made creed or law is the natural law of life -
the right of human individuals to live and to creatively express themselves. No man was born with the right to limit that law. Nor, do I
believe, can anyone justifiably work himself to such a position.

Down through the ages we have had various individuals doing their bit
to establish more securely these fundamental rights. They have tried
to help society see the necessity of understanding those fundamental
laws; some have succeeded to the extent of having these natural laws
recorded. Many have suffered unnatural deaths as a result of their
convictions. Yet, today, because of the efforts of some of these individuals, we have recorded in the laws of our nation certain rights
for all men, and certain additional rights for citizens. These fundamental moral rights and civil liberties are included in the Bill of
Rights, U. S. Constitution, and other legal records. They guarantee
that these fundamental rights shall not be denied without due process
of law.

The principles or the ideals are the things which give value to a person's life. They are the qualities which give impetus and purpose
toward meaningful experiences. The violation of human personality is
the violation of the most sacred thing which man owns.

This order for the mass evacuation of all persons of Japanese descent
denies them the right to live. It forces thousands of energetic, law-
abiding individuals to exist in a miserable psychological and a horrible
physical atmosphere. This order limits to almost full extent the creative
expressions of these subjected. It kills the desire for a higher life.
Hope for the future is exterminated. Human personalities are poisoned.
The very qualities which are essential to a peaceful, creative community
are being thrown out and abused. Over sixty per cent. are American citizens; yet they are denied on a wholesale scale without due process of
law the civil liberties which are theirs.

If I were to register and cooperate under those circumstances, I would
be giving helpless consent to the denial of practically all of the
things which give me incentive to live. I must maintain my Christian
principles. I consider it my duty to maintain the democratic standards
for which this nation lives. Therefore, I must refuse this order for
evacuation.

Let me add, however, that in refusing to register, I am well aware of
the excellent qualities of the Army and Government personnel connected
with the prosecution of this exclusion order. They are men of the finest
type and I sincerely appreciate their sympathetic and honest efforts.
Nor do I intend to cast any shadow upon the Japanese and the other Nisei
who have registered for evacuation. They have faced tragedy admirably.
I am objecting to the principle of this order which denies the rights
of human beings, including citizens.

Gordon K. Hirabayashi
May 13, 1942

(Mimeographed by Hirabayashi
Defense Fund Committee.)

On May 28, 1942, Hirabayashi was indicted for violating Public Law 505 that made the violation of the mandated curfew imposed upon Japanese-Americans a federal crime. He was subsequently arraigned on June 1, 1942, at which time he pleaded not guilty based upon the legal argument that both the exclusion law and the curfew denied him basic constitutional rights as a citizen of the United States.

He ultimately lost this case and was sentenced to serve his allotted time in confinement at a road camp and ended up at a camp outside of Tacoma, Washington. When Hirabayashi's legal team appealed this conviction to the Supreme Court, Hirabayashi v. United States, the justices by unanimous vote upheld his conviction on June 21, 1943.

He served his remaining time in a prison in Tucson, Arizona. There he met Hopi draft resistors and other pacifists like himself who refused military service on the grounds of being conscientious objectors. This experience reinforced his determination to resist.

Following his release from the federal prison in Tucson, he was faced with yet another challenge to his determination to resist what he believed were unconstitutional infringements on his personal liberty. He received a form from the Selective Service that came to be known as the "loyalty questionnaire (Form 304A). It was entitled, *The Statement of United States Citizens of Japanese Ancestry*

Since this form specifically singled out citizens of Japanese descent, he refused to fill it out and returned the blank form with a letter detailing his view regarding his view of the legitimacy of the questionnaire. His submission was ignored, and he was subsequently ordered to proceed to the CPS camp for induction. He refused induction. And was charged with Selective Service violations. In court, he represented himself, and was found guilty and was sentenced to one year at the McNeil Island Penitentiary.

After his release and following the end of the war, Hirabayashi completed his studies in sociology and with his advanced PhD degree, he taught abroad in Beirut, Lebanon, Cairo, Egypt, and Alberta Canada where he finally retired in 1983.

Ultimately, his wartime conviction was vacated by the Ninth Circuit Court of Appeals in 1987. This decision represented a repudiation of the extra-legal treatment of the Japanese-American population during the war.

In 1999, Hirabayashi was recognized for his courage and conviction in the face of the assault on his basic freedoms as a citizen of the United States by the renaming of the site of the Tucson Federal Prison in his honor to the *Gordon Hirabayashi Recreation Site*. In 2002, a kiosk was created that honored not only Hirabayashi, but also the forty-one Nisei draft resistors that were also sent to prison.

Hirabayashi died on January 2, 2012 and was subsequently posthumously awarded the Presidential Medal of Freedom by President Obama – a fitting acknowledgment to his contributions in living up to a central ideal of democracy – equal treatment of all under the law.

John Lewis

John Lewis (1940 – 2020) served in the United Congress for thirty-four years (seventeen terms) and was a tireless advocate for equality and justice for all. In addition to his career in national politics, Lewis had devoted his entire adult life to helping to establish true racial equality in the United States focusing his efforts in the American South where he was born and raised.

John Robert Lewis was born near the town of Troy, Alabama on February 21, 1940 in the midst of a culture dominated by Jim Crow – laws, ordinances and public policies that were designed to enforce segregation and deny African-Americans equal access to education, housing, employment and most importantly the ability to vote by creating formidable obstacles to that basic democratic right.

His parents were sharecroppers and he had to help his family through difficult times. Growing up, he had to witness the horrendous obstacles engineered to retard African progress through the machinations of Southern politics. He also witnessed first-hand the hard life of a Black sharecropper in that era. At an early age, he came to realize that this reality was neither right nor just.

He was fourteen years of age when the momentous decision by the Supreme Court in the landmark case of Brown v. the Board of Education (1954) ruled that separate was not equal and, therefore inherently unconstitutional. The young Lewis was particularly disappointed when it became apparent that this ruling would have no real impact upon his education.

In 1955 while Lewis was a fifteen-year-old, the Montgomery bus boycott of 1955 was an event that demonstrated the power of organized non-violent resistance. This development had a profound influence on Lewis and encouraged him to become more intimately involved in using direct action to implement change. He became involved in non-violent sit-ins at segregated lunch counters that exposed protesters to the violent reaction of local white populations that were inured to their dominant position within the social order.

In the fall of 1957, Lewis had the opportunity to attend the American Baptist Theological Seminary in Nashville Tennessee. It was an institution set up to train black ministers and was tuition free in exchange for working on campus. Once there he had the opportunity to listen to radio sermons from leaders in the growing civil rights movement and especially from Martin Luther King Jr. By the summer of 1958, he was invited to travel to Montgomery to meet with the Reverend Martin Luther King Jr. Soon, Lewis became thoroughly immersed in the civil rights movement especially inspired by the idea of using passive non-violent resistance to help bring about change. King was likewise inspired by the teachings and practice of Mahatma Gandhi who was instrumental in freeing India from British colonial rule.

Lewis became a Freedom Rider. The so-called "Freedom Rides" began in 1961 and were an organized attempt to challenge the segregation of riders of public transit that was prevalent in the South as a result of Jim Crow. This enforced segregation was imposed by local state governments in defiance of Supreme Court rulings - *Morgan v. Virginia* (1946) and *Boynton v. Virginia* (1960) - that clearly established the unconstitutionality of such laws in regard to travel on public transport. Participants in these freedom rides were frequently met with violence often at the hands of local police with the assistance of the Ku Klux Klan (KKK).

In 1963, Lewis became chairman of the Student Nonviolent Coordinating Committee (SNCC). As one of the planners of the March on Washington In August of 1963, Lewis was scheduled to give an address.

He gave a moving address that was mainly crafted by himself with the help of his colleagues at SNCC. The following is the text of that address before final revisions were made (taken from zinnedproject.org).

"We march today for jobs and freedom, but we have nothing to be proud of, for hundreds and thousands of our brothers are not here. They have no money for their transportation, for they are receiving starvation wages, or no wages at all.

"In good conscience, we cannot support wholeheartedly the administration's civil rights bill, for it is too little and too late. There's not one thing in the bill that will protect our people from police brutality.

"This bill will not protect young children and old women from police dogs and fire hoses, for engaging in peaceful demonstrations: This bill will not protect the citizens in Danville, Virginia, who must live in constant fear in a police state. This bill will not protect the hundreds of people who have been arrested on trumped up charges. What about the three young men in Americus, Georgia, who face the death penalty for engaging in peaceful protest?

"The voting section of this bill will not help thousands of black citizens who want to vote. It will not help the citizens of Mississippi, of Alabama and Georgia, who are qualified to vote but lack a sixth-grade education. "ONE MAN, ONE VOTE" is the African cry. It is ours, too. It must be ours.

"People have been forced to leave their homes because they dared to exercise their right to register to vote. What is there in this bill to ensure the equality of a maid who earns $5 a week in the home of a family whose income is $100,000 a year?

"For the first time in one hundred years this nation is being awakened to the fact that segregation is evil and that it must be destroyed in all forms. Your presence today proves that you have been aroused to the point of action.

"We are now involved in a serious revolution. This nation is still a place of cheap political leaders who build their careers on immoral compromises and ally themselves with open forms of political, economic, and social exploitation. What political leader here can stand up and say, "My party is the party of principles?" The party of Kennedy is also the party of Eastland. The party of Javits is also the party of Goldwater. Where is our party?

"In some parts of the South, we work in the fields from sunup to sundown for $12 a week. In Albany, Georgia, nine of our leaders have been indicted not by Dixiecrats but by the federal government for peaceful protest. But what did the federal government do when Albany's deputy sheriff beat attorney C. B. King and left him half dead? What did the federal government do when local police officials kicked and assaulted the pregnant wife of Slater King, and she lost her baby?

"It seems to me that the Albany indictment is part of a conspiracy on the part of the federal government and local politicians in the interest of expediency.

"I want to know, which side is the federal government on?

"The revolution is at hand, and we must free ourselves of the chains of political and economic slavery. The nonviolent revolution is saying, "We will not wait for the courts to act, for we have been waiting for hundreds of years. We will not wait for the President, the Justice Department, nor Congress, but we will take matters into our own hands and create a source of power, outside of any national structure, that could and would assure us a victory."

"To those who have said, "Be patient and wait," we must say that "patience" is a dirty and nasty word. We cannot be patient, we do not want to be free gradually. We want our freedom, and we want it now. We cannot depend on any political party, for both the Democrats and the Republicans have betrayed the basic principles of the Declaration of Independence.

"We all recognize the fact that if any radical social, political and economic changes are to take place in our society, the people, the masses, must bring them about. In the struggle, we must seek more than civil rights; we must work for the community of love, peace and true brotherhood. Our minds, souls and hearts cannot rest until freedom and justice exist for all people.

"The revolution is a serious one. Mr. Kennedy is trying to take the revolution out of the streets and put it into the courts. Listen, Mr. Kennedy. Listen, Mr. Congressman. Listen, fellow citizens. The black masses are on the march for jobs and freedom, and we must say to the politicians that there won't be a "cooling-off" period.

"All of us must get in the revolution. Get in and stay in the streets of every city, every village and every hamlet of this nation until true freedom comes, until the revolution is complete. In the Delta of Mississippi, in southwest Georgia, in Alabama, Harlem, Chicago, Detroit, Philadelphia and all over this nation, the black masses are on the march!

"We won't stop now. All of the forces of Eastland, Barnett, Wallace, and Thurmond won't stop this revolution. The time will come when we will not confine our marching to Washington. We will march through the South, through the heart of Dixie, the way Sherman did. We shall pursue our own scorched earth policy and burn Jim Crow to the ground — nonviolently. We shall fragment the South into a thousand pieces and put them back together in the image of democracy. We will make the action of the past few months look petty. And I say to you, WAKE UP AMERICA!"

The revision to this speech as outlined below came as a result of pressure from the administration of President John F. Kennedy and some of the more conservative speakers at the March. It indicated the necessity for some degree of compromise – "Cut were the words that criticized the President's bill as being "too little and too late." Lost was the call to march "through the heart of Dixie, the way Sherman did." Gone was the question asking, "which side is the federal government on?" The word "cheap" was removed to describe some political leaders. The ending of Lewis' speech as it was actually delivered is shown below:

"We will not stop. If we do not get meaningful legislation out of this Congress, the time will come when we will not confine our marching to Washington. We will march through the South, through the streets of Jackson, through the streets of Danville, through the streets of Cambridge, through the streets of Birmingham. But we will march with the spirit of love and with the spirit of dignity that we have shown here today.

"By the force of our demands, our determination, and our numbers, we shall splinter the desegregated South into a thousand pieces and put them back together in the image of God and democracy.

"We must say, "Wake up, America. Wake up!!! For we cannot stop, and we will not be patient."

The protestors that challenged the insidious nature of Jim Crow were of mixed race. One particular result of these demonstrations was the murder of Chaney, Goodman and Schwerner. These individuals were taken against their will in Neshoba County, Mississippi in June of 1964 and were subsequently murdered. Goodman and Schwerner were from New York City. They worked with the Council of Federated Organizations (COFO) and the Congress of Racial Equality (CORE). They were also involved in attempting to register African-Americans to vote. Since the end of Reconstruction that followed the Civil War, African-Americans were systematically prevented from registering to vote and ludicrous obstacles were in place to obstruct voting.

They had been arrested in Neshoba county for speeding. Following their release and before leaving Neshoba County, the three were abducted, and subsequently murdered. The men's bodies were later discovered in an earthen dam.

When this horrific news was reported to the nation, it aroused public anguish and outrage.

Following the March on Washington, the Civil Rights Act became law in 1964. However, this did not remove all the obstacles to voting in the American South. In response, Lewis and Hosea Williams planned and led a march from Selma to Montgomery, Alabama, on March 7, 1965. It became known as Bloody Sunday in Selma on account of the extreme violence that the peaceful demonstrators were subjected to.

In 2020, in a pilgrimage to the site of that horrific day in March in Selma, Lewis spoke the following words, "We took a little walk to try to dramatize the need for the rights of all of our people to be able to participate in the democratic process. In an orderly and peaceful fashion, we were walking, not saying a word. We were beaten. Tear gassed. Bullwhipped. On this bridge, some of us gave a little blood to help redeem the soul of America. Our country is a better country, we are a better people, but we still have a distance to travel, to go, before we get there. I want to thank each and every one of you for being here – for not giving up, for keeping the faith, for keeping your eyes on the prize."

In 2011, President Barack Obama presented Lewis with the Presidential Medal of Freedom.

In his seeming tireless pursuit of peace and social justice, Lewis organized a sit-in on the floor of the U.S. House of Representatives in response to the mass shooting in June of 2016 in Orlando Florida. This was done to draw attention to the need to craft legislation to curb gun violence that has taken the lives of so many innocent people.

In 2020, John Lewis died. He left behind a formidable legacy and demonstrated through his actions what is possible if individuals stand together with the intent of fashioning a better world for themselves and for all of humanity.

Chief Joseph of the Nez Perce

Chief Joseph of the Nez Perce was known to his people as "Thunder Traveling to the Loftier Mountain Heights."

The Nez Perce occupied an area of Oregon referred to as the Wallowa valley in Eastern Oregon. These people were first exposed to white settlers during the Lewis and Clark expedition (1804 – 1806). They were treated with kindness, consideration, and compassion. On this first encounter they were impressed by the technological advances and capabilities of these strangers. To some members of the Nez Perce people, they were regarded as superior beings whom they wanted to emulate. This embrace of these newcomers, however, would prove to be of relatively short duration.

It was not long after this initial encounter, that the NEZ Perce people were visited by Christian missionaries. An example was that of Henry and Eliza Spalding. It was during the mid-nineteenth century that missionaries set out to settle in the West with the idea of disseminating Christianity and educating Native American tribes in the Pacific Northwest. Henry and Eliza Spalding set out with Narcissa and Marcus Whitman in February of 1836 from New York to preach to Native American tribes. Twelve or fifteen members of the Nez Perce Tribe greeted them in July of that year and "received them gladly," according to a letter published by Henry Spalding. The Nez Perce tribe magnanimously gifted them horses and supported their endeavor until the Spaldings and Whitmans parted ways in October 1836. The Spaldings remained with the Nez Perce tribe and finally settled in the Lapwai Valley, becoming the first Christian missionaries among the Nez Perce. An exposure to the ways of the white man as exemplified by the lifestyle of these missionaries led many Nez Perce to convert to Christianity. Joseph's father, Tuekakas, as chief of the Nez Perce was a convert to Christianity and as a consequence, Joseph was exposed at an early age to the ways, customs and beliefs of these foreigners.

Although the fact that the homeland of the Nez Perce was remote and hard to reach initially served as a significant barrier to encroachment by white settlers, this protection was disrupted by two significant events in the early history of the U.S. republic. One was the California

Gold Rush of 1848 and the other was Homestead Act of 1862 that granted up to 160 acres of land to those white settlers who would establish residence and make the land productive. This act resulted in the settlement of about 1.6 million white settlers on land mostly West of the Mississippi.

Although many individuals migrated to California In search of gold, few became rich. When the dream of making one's fortune withered, many were attracted to the West as a place to settle. As a result, these erstwhile prospectors began to encroach upon the land of the Nez Perce.

In addition, the push to settle in the vast lands of the West promoted by the Federal government through the enactment of the Homestead Act was hampered by the presence of Native American populations that were already resident. In the face of this reality, the government attempted to come to some kind of peaceful arrangement with these populations through the instrument of treaties. However, there was no real incentive to honor the provisions of these treaties, since the newly formed American nation possessed a superiority in numbers and military capability. The historic record is replete with examples of the abrogation of these treaty arrangements.

When Joseph became chief following the death of his father, Tuekakas, he naively believed that the U.S. was sincere in its efforts to find peaceful arrangements and would be true to treaty obligations. It is important to understand that the Nez Perce had a strong body of spiritual beliefs in which the land and all that resided upon it were considered a sacred and sustaining aspect of existence and could not be owned, purchased, or exploited. In this light, the attitudes and politics of the white settlers and the U.S. government seemed wholly inexplicable.

The turning point in this tenuous relationship came In 1877 as a result of the conference held between many of the indigenous tribal leaders and General Howard representing the U.S. government. The meeting was held at Fort Lapwai. It was Howard's intention to use this opportunity to issue an ultimatum to those invited Native American leaders that they must leave their land and move to designated reservations. They could do this freely or be forced to migrate. The outcome of this conference demonstrated once and for all the unwillingness of the United States government to honor its treaty obligations when it was not in its interest to do so. The ultimate conclusion of this conference was that Howard issued his ultimatum that the Nez Perce must either move out of their homeland to a reservation defined by the U.S. government within thirty days or be forcefully driven out. When Chief Joseph attempted to suggest that this abbreviated timeline was impossible to adhere to, his entreaties were ignored.

Rather than accept this ultimatum, Chief Joseph fled with his people – there goal was to travel to Canada and remove themselves entirely from jurisdiction of the U.S. government. This journey represented a 1400 mile trek (see map on the following page) while constantly being pursued by the U.S. army. This was a brave yet futile effort that resulted in the death of many hundreds of his people. He ultimately surrendered in 1877.

Following the final defeat of the Nez Perce at the hands of the pursuing forces, Chief Joseph gave a very poignant and unforgettable speech on October 5, 1877, upon his surrender to General Howard who had been assaulting him and his people for many months in their vain attempt to flee to freedom in Canada. His speech is shown below.

"I am tired of fighting. Our chiefs are killed. Looking Glass is dead. Toohoolhoolzote is dead. The old men are all dead. It is the young men who say, 'Yes' or 'No.' He who led the young men [Olikut] is dead. It is cold, and we have no blankets. The little children are freezing to death. My people, some of them, have run away to the hills, and have no blankets, no food. No one knows where they are — perhaps freezing to death. I want to have time to look for my children and see how many of them I can find. Maybe I shall find them among the dead. Hear me, my chiefs! I am tired. My heart is sick and sad. From where the sun now stands I will fight no more forever."

It is a testament to his timeless courage and unshakeable conviction that there is a town in Oregon (Joseph, Oregon) near Wallowa Lake named after him and the Nez Perce Memorial National Park was created in the same region that is also the site where he is buried. Of course, whether or not the descendants of the Nez Perce will ever be justly compensated for the grave injustice perpetrated against their people is an open question.

The story of this remarkable human being is an extraordinary one and serves as a stunning indictment of the brutality and horrific treatment afforded the native peoples of the expansive territory of the United States by the newly formed nation in its pursuit of expansion and social, economic, and political hegemony.

Stacey Abrams

Stacey Abrams has established herself as a significant force for change especially in regard to the political rights of African-Americans in the nation in general and in her native state of Georgia in particular. She is a rising star within the Democratic Party having served in the Georgia House of Representatives for eleven years and became her party's nominee for the governorship of Georgia. In the 2018 election, she lost by a very close margin – gaining 48.8 % of the popular vote. Serious questions arose regarding the management of the election by the Georgia Office of the Secretary State – the head of this department was her Republican Party opponent, Brian Kemp. Kemp resigned his post as Secretary of State following the election.

The following is the full text of Abrams "concession" speech following the final election vote count that clearly

Voices for Peace and Social Justice Volume 3 demonstrates her concerns about the actual conduct of the election process.

"In September 18, thousands of Georgians began casting absentee ballots, determined to lift their voices in the democratic process of electing our leaders for the next two years, the next four years. A few weeks later, more than two million Georgians declared their choices, heading to polling places for early votes. Then, on November 6, more than a million folks arrived in precincts around our beloved state – anxious and excited to express their patriotism through the basic, fundamental act of voting.

"For these millions of Georgians, the act may have proven tedious and hard, but they had no doubts their votes would be counted. Certainly, there would be long lines and delays. Absolutely, a tired volunteer would mistype a name. And Nature would not be ignored – through rain or tornado warning or chilly weather.

"We all understand challenges and complications; however, this year, more than two hundred years into Georgia's democratic experiment, the state failed its voters. You see, despite a record high population in Georgia, more than a million citizens found their names stripped from the rolls by the Secretary of State, including a 92 year-old civil rights activist who had cast her ballot in the same neighborhood since 1968. Tens of thousands hung in limbo, rejected due to human error and a system of suppression that had already proven its bias. The remedy, they were told, was simply to show up – only they, like thousands of others, found polling places shut down, understaffed, ill-equipped or simply unable to serve its basic function for lack of a power cord.

"Students drove hours to hometowns to cast votes because mismanagement prevented absentee ballots from arriving on time. Parents stood in the fitful rain in four-hour lines, watching as less fortunate voters had to abandon democracy in favor of keeping their jobs. Eligible voters were refused ballots because poll workers thought they didn't have enough paper to go around. Ballots were rejected by the handwriting police. Georgia citizens tried to exercise their constitutional rights and were still denied the ability to elect their leaders. Under the watch of the now former Secretary of State, democracy failed Georgians of every political party, every race, every region. Again.

"The incompetence and mismanagement we witnessed in this election had been on display months before—in the Republican state legislative primary of Dan Gasaway. Counties, under the direction of the Secretary of State, issued flawed ballots – and not for the first time and not just there. But this time, the mistakes clearly altered the outcome. Rep. Gasaway, a Republican in a heavily Republican district, had to go to court to force a fair fight. Therefore, on December 4, tucked between run-offs for Secretary of State and the Public Service Commission, for one community, there will be justice in the process. Win or lose, the people in his district will finally have a say.

"Many of the same Republicans who cheered on Rep. Gasaway as he filed his lawsuit have grumbled about the time we have taken to gain a remedy for fellow Georgians who faced a dizzying array of bad action, misinformation and gut-wrenching hardship.

"But we are a mighty nation because we embedded in our national experiment the chance to fix what is broken. To call out what has faltered. To demand fairness wherever it can be found. Which is why on Election Night, I declared that our fight to count every vote is not about me. It is about us. It's about the democracy we share and our responsibility to preserve our way of life. Our democracy—because voting is a right and not a privilege.

"I stand here today as witness to that truth. This election is about all of us—as is the resolution of this moment.

"I acknowledge that former Secretary of State Brian Kemp will be certified as the victor in the 2018 gubernatorial election.

"But to watch an elected official—who claims to represent the people of this state, baldly pin his hopes for election on the suppression of the people's democratic right to vote—has been truly appalling. So, to be clear, this is not a speech of concession.

"Concession means to acknowledge an action is right, true or proper. As a woman of conscience and faith, I cannot concede. But my assessment is that the law currently allows no further viable remedy.

"Now, I could certainly bring a new case to keep this one contest alive, but I don't want to hold public office if I need to scheme my way into the post. Because the title of Governor isn't nearly as important as our shared title. Voters.

"And this is why we fight on and why I want to say thank you. Thank you for organizing your communities and shattering records – more than 1.9 million voters who stood up for protecting our public schools, continued criminal justice reform, Medicaid expansion and real economic mobility for all of our counties. We won state House races and Senate races, a new seat in Congress and put America on notice that change is not coming – it has arrived. And you made it so.

"But those who fear change pushed back, and so we waited for the whole truth of this election – good and evil – to come forth. So thank you sharing your stories, for the tens of thousands of calls into our voter protection line. Thank you for volunteering your hours after the polls closed and for the past ten days. For driving to all 159 counties and for hearing the concerns of Georgia citizens, through tears and frustration and disappointment.

"Because Georgia still has a decision to make about who will we be in the next election. And the one after that. And the one after that. So we have used this election and its aftermath to diagnose what has been broken in our process:

"Make no mistake, the former Secretary of State was deliberate and intentional in his actions. I know that eight years of systemic disenfranchisement, disinvestment and incompetence had its desired effect on the electoral process in Georgia.

"I also know that we live in a nation where four federal judges were necessary to force the counting of more ballots cast, in the face of Brian Kemp's opposition and disregard to their lawful consideration.

"I know that millions of Georgians, of Americans – of goodwill and various partisan beliefs – are enraged by these truths. In response, you may seek to vent your anger, or worse, turn away from politics because it can be as rigged and rotten as you've always believed.

"I implore each of you to not give in to that anger or apathy but instead turn to action. Because the antidote to injustice is progress. The cure to this malpractice is a fight for fairness in every election held – in every law passed – in every decision made.

"Pundits and hyper-partisans will hear my words as a rejection of the normal order. I'm supposed to say nice things and accept my fate. They will complain that I should not use this moment to recap what was done wrong or to demand a remedy. As a leader, I should be stoic in my outrage and silent in my rebuke.

"But stoicism is a luxury and silence is a weapon for those who would quiet the voices of the people, and I will not concede because the erosion of our democracy is not right.

"Regardless of party, we want what is best for our children, for our families, for our neighborhoods. We may not share the same faith, but we are knitted together by our belief in our potential for more. I will work in these coming weeks to elect John Barrow as our next Secretary of State – a man of principle and goodwill who will administer his responsibilities for the people – not his party. I will work to elect Lindy Miller as our next Public Service Commissioner, where she will speak for those who have been ignored for too long.

"And I will pray for the success of Brian Kemp, that he will indeed be a leader for all Georgians. That he will pledge to fight for the rights of those who disagree with him – and keep his promises. That he will refuse the call of those who see how close this election was. Because we know that some propose to make voting even harder. They see voter engagement in communities of color and cry fraud or lie about the cost of democracy to justify closing more polling places. I pray he will reject this vicious and tired response – in favor of preserving what is left of our state's reputation for equality and civil rights.

"But I will not leave it to prayers alone. As I have for more than twenty years, I will stand with my fellow Georgians in pursuit of fairness. I did so as a college student speaking in the shadow of Lincoln and King at the 30th anniversary of the March on Washington. I did so as the Democratic Leader of the House and as the Democratic nominee for Governor of Georgia. And I will do so as a private citizen, ready to continue to defend those whose choices were denied their full expression.

"Today, I announce the launch of Fair Fight Georgia, an operation that will pursue accountability in Georgia's elections and integrity in the process of maintaining our voting rolls. In the coming days, we will be filing a major federal lawsuit against the state of Georgia for the gross mismanagement of this election and to protect future elections from unconstitutional actions.

"We will channel the work of the past several weeks into a strong legal demand for reform of our elections system in Georgia. And I will not waver in my commitment to work across party lines and across divisions to find a common purpose in protecting our democracy. For a state that elects Democrats and Republicans and Independents.

That elects leaders who will not tolerate an erosion of our values.

"Fair Fight Georgia. Because these votes are our voices. We are each entitled to our choices. And we have always, Georgia, been at the forefront of speaking truth to whatever power may lay claim to leadership – if only for the moment. We will win because we are Georgia.

"And we will get it done."

Fair Fight subsequently filed a lawsuit that alleged that state election officials "grossly mismanaged an election that deprived Georgia citizens, and particularly citizens of color, of their fundamental right to vote."

The complaint, filed in U.S. District Court, cited issues from sweeping purges of the voter rolls to shuttered precincts, voting equipment failures and late absentee ballots.

It highlighted stories of voters who said they were turned away from the polls under state requirements that their personal information on voter applications match state databases exactly. Many voters also experienced long waits at polling places that lacked sufficient provisional ballots as a backup.

In preparation for the general election of 2020, Abrams was instrumental in creating Fair Fight 2020 with the goal of funding a program to train "voter protection teams" in 20 battleground states. She contributed a great deal of her energy to protecting and preserving voting rights, and in 2019 she initiated a program referred to as, "Fair Count" to monitor the accuracy of the 2020 Census.

Abrams was born in Madison, Wisconsin in 1973. She is one of six children in her family, grew up in Gulfport, Mississippi and spent her formative years in Georgia. She is a woman with many talents - with degrees from Spelman College, the LBJ School of Public Affairs at the University of Texas and Yale Law School.

Abrams is also impassioned in the arena of international relations. In recognition of her work in this field, she has served on the Subcommittee on Diversity on the Council on Foreign Relations. Abrams is a Next Generation Fellow of the American Assembly on U.S. Global Policy and the Future of International Institutions.

Abram's interests are global in scope. She has been a Fellow on many international projects including East Asian Studies, American Marshall Memorial, American Council of Young Political Leaders, Council on Italy, the British-American Project and U.S.-Russian Young Leaders. As a result, she had traveled extensively.

Abrams is also the recipient of the John F. Kennedy New Frontier Award, and a member of the Board of Directors for the Center for American progress. She represents her generation exceedingly well – forward looking, inclusive, dedicated to civil rights issues not only within the United States but globally as well.

Abrams' dedication, energy, and resourcefulness especially in the area of voting rights has established her reputation as an eloquent advocate for democratic principles. Her efforts in getting out the vote in the general election of 2020 has proven to be invaluable in contributing to the ultimate outcome.

Raif Badawi

Raif bin Muhammad Badawi gained notoriety when he was arrested in 2012 at the age of twenty-eight for the following crimes: "setting up a website that undermines general security", "ridiculing Islamic religious figures", and "going beyond the realm of obedience." He was sentenced to seven years in prison. This sentence was increased to 10 years in 2014.

Badawi is a is a Saudi writer actively engaged in advocating for a more liberal social and political environment in his native Saudi Arabia. To expand his audience, he created a website – *Free Saudi Liberals*.

Badawi's blog had many members. It quickly became a forum for vigorous debate regarding Saudi politics. For this reason, he was arrested in late 2007. Although he was eventually released, he became the victim of constant harassment that eventually led to his subsequent arrest in 2012.

Raif Badawi was born on January 13, 1984, in Khobar, Saudi Arabia. His parents are Najwa, a Lebanese Christian, and Muhammad Badawi, a Saudi Muslim. At a young age, his Saudi grandmother explained to him that, "Saudi society historically was not as strict and men and women used to work together in the fields."

Badawi's mother died young at an unknown age. He was raised by his father and grandmother in a household beset by economic difficulties. Badawi attended school until the age of thirteen when his father reported him for parental disobedience, a crime in Saudi Arabia, and spent six months in a teenage detention center.

Saudi Arabia is a theocratic monarchy whose laws and regulations follow the rulings and teaching of Islamic law. The legal system is based on sharia as interpreted by Sunni Islamic jurisprudence. The government is under the leadership of a king and prime minister. Furthermore, the royal family rules by fiat, and there is no Constitution.

Wahhabism is an Islamic revisionist theology that exerts a powerful influence in Saudi Arabian politics. It derived its name from the teachings of Muhammad ibn Abd al-Wahhabi. Wahhabism is an extremely stringent and uncompromising from of Islam that insists on a purely literal interpretation of the Koran. Through this highly restrictive interpretation, those who do not practice this form of Islam are considered heathens and are dealt with harshly. In Saudi Arabia apostasy itself is considered a crime worthy of the death penalty.

Badawi was influenced by the writings of progressive Arab author, Abdullah al-Qasemi, and Turki al-Hamad, a noted journalist and thinker. He was particularly inspired by Mohammed Saeed Tayeb, a staunch believer in democracy who was also imprisoned.

Ultimately, he became so concerned about the oppressive and authoritarian nature of Saudi politics that he began to speak out openly in regard to these concerns. For this reason, Badawi's activities were considered by the government as anathema and explains the severity of the punishment he has been forced to endure. Badawi's courageous insistence on expressing his views has been regarded as a particular threat, for the government's autocratic imposition of Islam on the lives of its people is especially vulnerable in the human world of the twenty-first century in which global communication is a predominant aspect of modern life.

He has been reported to be in poor health, and his general condition has noticeably worsened during his imprisonment and torture according to his wife, Ensaf Haidar, currently residing in Canada. She fled her native country convinced that her life would be endangered if she remained in Saudi Arabia.

The following interview with Ensaf Haidar was conducted by Jaafar Abdul Karim at Deutshe Welle (dw.com) in 2017.

Ensaf Haidar: The fact that my husband has been in jail for five years shows that there is no freedom of expression in Saudi Arabia.

Raif expressed his opinion in a friendly and peaceful manner, so there was no reason to be afraid. He had also written for Saudi newspapers, and that shows that he wasn't an enemy of the state. He even had the experience of traveling abroad.

So why are some states so afraid of these independent spirits?

Because of the different opinions. It's us they're afraid of, not the expression of opinion as such.

So they would prefer there to be only one opinion?

This is what their approach suggests. They want everyone to be of the same opinion. They're afraid of a wide range of opinions.

How is your husband doing at the moment?

After five years in captivity separated from his children and the outside world, he's naturally doing poorly physically and psychologically. He has been imprisoned for five years without having committed a crime.

Of course, the Saudi authorities see the situation differently. What do you tell your children? Do they understand what's going on?

They understand it and are proud of their father, though they miss him very much. They need him, especially at this age.

Do you stay in constant contact with Raif?

In the beginning he always called me for brief periods of time, but I haven't heard anything from him in over three weeks.

If we had press freedom, Raif would be free. He's been in jail for five years and he'll be there for five more. Along with that he's also been handed a 10-year travel ban, a fine of one million riyal ($266,654 USD) and 1,000 lashings by cane. Anyone who sees this sentence can decide if we have press freedom here or not.

How important then is freedom of expression?

There are people who say there is already too much division; there's terrorism and there's foreign interference, which undermine a country's sovereignty.

Those who speak peacefully and know the laws have the right to express themselves! That is a basic right of every person, whatever the subject.

Do you speak with your children about freedom of expression?

That is a social issue and not just a legal one. From society as well there is a partial rejection of freedom of expression…

Here in Canada it is, of course, completely different. It's a secular country, where you can express your opinion freely, directly in the press. When I tell my kids about their father, they don't understand what the problem is at all with someone having a blog. It's completely different here.

There is an international solidarity campaign for your husband. How does that make you feel?

I can only be thankful and hope that the initiators continue with it. However, so far it has had a psychological effect. It hasn't impacted the proceedings against Raif so far. But I hope that the solidarity continues nonetheless, because moral support is so important. That gives Raif and me hope and strength.

Do you personally hope that pressure from the campaign will help free Raif? It is now an international campaign.

I hope that the Saudi government one day recognizes that freedom of expression is every man's right. Raif always peacefully expressed himself and loved his country. In this way I hope that he soon comes free.

What is your appeal for World Press Freedom Day?

I hope that the whole world continues to stand by us. I call on the Saudi government to give every citizen a space for freedom of expression.

Badawi is currently represented by The Raoul Wallenberg Centre for Human Rights that acts as his international legal counsel. The mission statement of this organization is the following as presented on their website (raoulwallenbergcentre.org).

"The Raoul Wallenberg Centre for Human Rights is a unique international consortium of parliamentarians, scholars, jurists, human rights defenders, NGOs, and students united in the pursuit of justice, inspired by and anchored in Raoul Wallenberg's humanitarian legacy – how act can confront evil, prevail, and transform history.

"From mid-May to early July 1944, the Nazis deported 440,000 from Hungary to the Auschwitz Birkenau death camp – one of the most efficient, cruelest, and most horrific mass deportations in the Holocaust. Raoul Wallenberg arrived as a Swedish diplomat in the Swedish legation in Budapest in July 1944 and in six months saved 100,000 Jews.

"The Wallenberg Centre is organized around five pillars of pursuing justice, each of which reflects and represents Wallenberg's humanitarian legacy. The Honorary Co-Chairs of the Raoul Wallenberg Centre for Human Rights are: Nobel Peace Laureate Elie Wiesel (U.S. – in memoriam); the Honorable Justice Rosalie Abella (Supreme Court of Canada); the Honourable Göran Persson (former Prime Minister of Sweden); and the Honourable Elyakim Rubinstein (Former Deputy President of the Israeli Supreme Court). The Centre's Founder and International Chair is Professor Irwin Cotler and the Co-Chairs from countries of Wallenberg's Honorary Citizenship include

Jared Genser (US); Michael Danby (Australia); and Natan Sharansky (Israel)."

The goal of this organization is to use the global media as well as private diplomatic efforts to help secure Badawi's release from prison.

According to this organization, "Raif Badawi has been languishing in a Saudi prison since his arrest in 2012, and his subsequent sentencing in 2014 to 10 years imprisonment and 1000 lashes, itself constitutive of torture and a standing violation of International Human Rights Law. Badawi's "crime"? Establishing an online forum and exercising his right to freedom of expression. Despite Saudi Arabia expressing an interest in reforming and modernizing, Raif Badawi – an advocate of liberalism and tolerance, and the champion of these changes – remains imprisoned and separated from his wife and three children, now citizens of Canada."

While his exact location is unknown, it has been reported that Badawi is currently imprisoned in Dhahban Central Prison.

Following the 2012 arrest, Amnesty International designated Badawi a prisoner of conscience. As reported on their website – amnestyusa.org,

"In May 2014, Raif Badawi was sentenced to 10 years behind bars, 1,000 lashes, a 10-year travel ban, and a lifetime ban from appearing in the media. He was convicted of violating Saudi Arabia's draconian information technology law and "insulting Islam." The conviction stems from number of articles Raif wrote and published on his site "Saudi Arabian Liberals," which he founded as a forum for social and political debate. Raif also refused to remove other Saudi writers' articles from the site.

"We want life for those who call for our death, and rationality for those who desire ignorance for us." -Raif Badawi

"The charges against Raif are related to articles he wrote criticizing religious authorities in Saudi Arabia, and pieces penned by others that Raif published on the Saudi Arabian Liberals' site. The prosecution had called for him to be tried for 'apostasy' or abandoning his religion, which carries the death penalty.

"Raif is one of many activists in Saudi Arabia persecuted for openly expressing their views online. Facebook and Twitter are incredibly popular in a country where people can't openly voice their opinions in public. The authorities have responded to this increase in online debate by monitoring social media sites and even trying to ban applications such as Skype and WhatsApp, further stifling free expression."

Badawi's unshakeable determination and remarkable courage as an advocate of human freedom and the right to express one's views openly are of great value to us all, and a reminder of the inherent power of the human spirit.

Sarah Deer

On May 28, 2020, Sarah Deer gave the keynote address for the virtual graduation ceremonies at Brooklyn College. The following is taken from the school's website in the reporting of this event:

"The Class of 2020 drew more inspiration from keynote speaker, Dr. Sarah Deer, who President Anderson presented with an honorary Doctor of Humane Letters in recognition of her outstanding contributions to human rights and especially to the rights of indigenous women.

"A professor of public policy from the University of Kansas and a member of the Muscogee (Creek) Nation, Deer has worked for more than 25 years to end violence against women. She was named a MacArthur Fellow in 2014 and is a recent recipient of an Andrew Carnegie fellowship. Deer is a co-author of four textbooks on tribal law. Her work on violence against Native women has received national recognition from the American Bar Association and the Department of Justice. She is also the Chief Justice for the Prairie Island Indian Community Court of Appeals.

"Opening her welcoming remarks in her native Mvskoke language, Deer told the Class of 2020 she also recognized the extraordinary commitment and sacrifice the entire class made earning their degrees. Urging the recent graduates to always fight for what is important to them, Deer told the story of the first Native American woman to practice before the United States Supreme Court, Lyda Conley, who fought for decades to save her people's cemetery located in Kansas in the early part of the 20th century. A member of the Wyandot Tribe in Kansas, Conley graduated from the Kansas City School of Law in 1902, to become the first woman admitted to the Kansas Bar. She then battled the Department of the Interior and the Supreme Court to eventually save the hallowed ground, sometimes physically guarding it for 24 hours a day.

"As a Native attorney myself, I have looked to Lyda's story with fascination and appreciation," Deer said. "While my legal career has not involved guarding a cemetery, I have found that creativity is sometimes the key to finding justice."

Deer left the Class of 2020 with three thoughts: "Take risks, take care of yourself, and when you identify something that makes you passionate, don't dismiss it as a pie-in-the-sky aspiration—figure out a way to make it work, because you know it won't happen if you give up."

Deer has been a persistent and outspoken voice against violence towards women ever since her days as an undergraduate student at the University of Kansas where she volunteered to serve as an advocate for women who were rape victims. She later went on to pursue a law degree specializing in those legal issues unique to Native-American women who were rape survivors.

Once she received a law degree, Deer joined the faculty of the Mitchell Hamline School of Law (2008). She currently serves as an appellate judge for the Prairie Island Indian Community Court of Appeals and the White Earth Nation Court of Appeals in Minnesota.

Deer has co-authored a number of notable textbooks centering on tribal law and in 2015 her book entitled, *The Beginning and End of Rape: Confronting Sexual Violence in Native America*, was published. Her accomplishments include the Allied Professional Award from the United States Department of Justice for her well-recognized efforts in behalf of victims' issues (2011) and in 2014 she became a MacArthur Fellow – a prestigious position.

Deer has devoted her professional life and energy to advocacy against violence perpetrated to the detriment of women especially among the Native American population. This is an issue of great importance that does not get the kind of coverage in the media that it certainly deserves.

The fact that Deer has chosen to serve as an eloquent judicial advocate for the plight of Native American women in the United States not only reflects upon her own character and commitment, but also represents the strides that have been made in recent decades in regard to Native-American civil rights.

Joseph Aprile   Sarah Deer

It is encouraging to realize that there is a broad-based awakening among native people not only in the United States but around the world to the reality of their own significance and their inherent human and ethnic rights.

Dame Cicely Saunders

Cicely Mary Strode Saunders, was the founder of the modern conception of hospice and, also established the discipline and rigor associated with palliative care – a type of care with the primary goal of relieving pain and distress in patients with severe and often terminal illnesses. By definition, a hospice is a home for the severely or terminally ill patient.

Cicely Mary Strode Saunders was born in Barnet, Hertfordshire, England in 1918. She was the eldest of three children. Saunders' family was financially well-situated; however, the household environment was deeply affected by a controlling father and a remote and withdrawn mother. The family lived in in a large house with spacious grounds.

When Saunders was just one years old, she was cared for by her Aunt Daisy. This arrangement was soon abruptly ended and she was subsequently returned to her home and sent to Roedean School when she was 10 years-old. At school, Saunders was taller than the other girls. This difference made her feel awkward and separate from her peers. she felt that this aspect of her growing up made her come to appreciate those who were considered different. As a child Saunders suffered from scoliosis – defined as a sideways curvature of the spine - severe enough that she was made to lie flat on the floor for 40 minutes a day.

These experiences as a child may have contributed to her desire to be of service to others and become a nurse. Her father did not approve of this choice of possible careers. As a result, she went to St. Anne's College in Oxford where she pursued the study of politics, philosophy, and economics with the goal of eventually working in government.

However, the outbreak of World War II that began when Germany - under the aegis of Adolph Hitler - invaded Poland (1939), disrupted this career path, and, defying her father's wishes, she enrolled as a student at The Nightingale Training School to become a Red Cross war nurse. During her training, she had rotations at several mental hospitals and worked at the Park Prewett Hospital in London. Physically, the work was very stressful, and placed an additional burden on her back. As a result, she returned to Oxford for a year and gained a "war degree." She was trained at the Royal Cancer Hospital that qualified her as a social worker (almoner), in 1947.

It was in the following year that a life-changing experience altered the course of her professional career.

While working at Archway hospital in London, she cared for a Polish émigré, David Tasma, who was dying. In the course of her caregiving, Saunders and Tasma became intensely involved with each other. In their conversations, the idea occurred to them of founding a home in which people who were dying could find some solace and peace in their final days. On his death, he left her 500 pounds as seed money to realize this dream.

Saunders was advised by professional colleagues that if she truly wished to realize her dream, she should obtain a degree in medicine as a doctor. It was reasoned that with this credential she would be more readily listened to. In 1957, she became a physician graduating from St. Thomas' Medical School in London. She broadened her knowledge in pharmacology so that she could better understand how to alleviate pain in terminally ill patients. With this knew knowledge, she became a powerful advocate for the regular administration of pain medications to such patients rather than supplying them on demand.

In 1958, shortly after she qualified, she wrote an article concerning a new approach to the end of life. In it she stated that, "It appears that many patients feel deserted by their doctors at the end. Ideally the doctor should remain the centre of a team who work together to relieve where they cannot heal, to keep the patient's own struggle within his compass and to bring hope and consolation to the end."

During this time, Saunders began to formulate her vision for a facility devoted to the care of terminally-ill patents. She envisioned a facility that would provide emotional and spiritual support in addition to the traditional focus on medicine. She also appreciated the value of providing a comforting and homelike environment to those at the end of life. Saunders also kept in mind the need to offer support to the families of patients as well, recognizing the stressful aspects of end-of-life issues.

By 1959, she had drawn up a detailed proposal for the hospice she had in mind. After an intense period of negotiation, construction began in 1965 – it was to be called St. Christopher's Hospice located in South London. It was opened in 1967. It has since become a prime model for hospice care to this date, that is emulated throughout the world.

Saunders spent her final days at St. Christopher's along with her husband, Marian Bohusz-Szyszko. He passed away in 1995 and she continued working until the end of her life in 2005.

The extent of the contribution Saunder's has made to the caring of the terminally ill might best be expressed in her own words taken as an excerpt from her acceptance address of the Templeton Prize given on May 12, 1981.

"For over 1,000 years hospice was a resting place for pilgrims, giving them a welcome that lasted till they were ready to go on. For a few, the sick and wounded, it would have been the last stage. For the past 100 years or so hospice has also meant a foundation, still religious, admitting those with incurable illness when the hospitals would no longer care for them. Founded on both sides of the Atlantic and in Australia around the turn of the century, they were for patients dying of cancer and of tuberculosis and with long term illness when the only alternatives were the Poor Law and similar Institutions. Among this group it was the Irish Sisters of Charity who chose the name Hospice, first in Dublin, later in Hackney and applied it especially to those who were dying.

"Over the past decade the word has been filled up with new meanings and has come to stand for a world-wide movement identified by attitudes and expertise rather than by bricks and mortar, for many hospice teams have no beds of their own. *I would define the modern hospice as a skilled community working to improve the quality of life remaining for patients and their families struggling with mortal and long-term illness. Some also include the frail elderly. Hospice is about a special kind of living and in a sense is still concerned with travelling: patients, families, elderly residents and the staff and volunteers who meet them, find they are drawn into a journey of the spirit.*

"However, this new development began with a building when you, Ma'am, opened St. Christopher's in July 1967, when we took the word Hospice from St. Joseph's, generous in this as in everything else. Not the first hospice, but the first planned not only to care for a mixed group of patients but also to develop research and teaching."

Joseph Aprile   Dame Cicely Saunders

It is for these reasons that the name and person of Dame Cicely Saunders has become synonymous with what is regarded as modern hospice care. Without her clear and compassionate vision, the pain and suffering endured by the terminally ill would not have been so effectively curtailed.

Anne Hutchinson

Anne Hutchinson, born Anne Marbury and baptized July 20, 1591, in Alford, Lincolnshire, England. She was to play a pivotal role in the development and growth of the Puritan community's presence in the New World – Massachusetts Bay Colony.

In order to fully recognize her influence, it is important to appreciate the historic context of her time. During the 16th century religion played an essential role in European politics. In 1534 King Henry the VIII of England upended the dominance of the Catholic Church in English life by founding the Church of England (Anglican Church). This schism came about as a result of a personal dispute after Pope Clement VII refused to grant him permission to marry Anne Boleyn.

This challenge to the excesses of papal authority was echoed in Germany by the inception of the Protestant Reformation Inspired by Martin Luther (1517). Within England the spirit of questioning of religious belief spawned a movement within the Church of England referred to as Puritanism. Puritans adopted a more rigorous application of the teachings of the Bible in daily life and were more stoic in their general demeanor.

Anne Marbury was the daughter of Francis Marbury a renegade Anglican clergyman who abandoned the use of ornate vestments and other manifestations of what he considered to be remnants of papal influence. He became such a vocal critic of the Anglican Church, that in 1578 he was taken into custody by church authorities and he was finally convicted of heresy and was sent to prison for two years.

In 1582, he married Elizabeth Moore, but after only four years of marriage, she died. Over his lifetime, Marbury had some twenty children; many of his descendants became important figures in the history of the United States including the poet John Dryden, U.S. Senator Mitt Romney as well as Franklin Delano Roosevelt, George H.W. Bush and George W. Bush.

His daughter Anne was born during her father's house arrest that began in 1590; for he was unwilling to remain silent regarding his ongoing criticism of the Anglican Church. There is, however, no official record of her birth except her date of baptism in 1591. The young Anne was home-schooled along with her many siblings. Surprisingly, nineteen of the purported twenty children survived even within an environment imperiled by the Black Plague - from

1592 to 1593, London experienced its last major plague outbreak of the 16th century .

Marbury was determined to teach all of his children, regardless of gender, to be well-educated adults capable of exerting a positive impact on their culture. Anne grew up in Alford, a small town, and attended religious services at St. Wilfrid's parish church where she heard about a charismatic preacher, John Cotton, from the nearby town of Boston, England. Cotton was a Puritan like Anne and emphasized the importance of faith and conversion to Christ and the role of grace in religious life. This school of religious thought was referred to as covenant theology. Anne was greatly influenced by this outspoken and charismatic minister.

Once Marbury was allowed to preach once again, he and his family moved to London where he developed quite a reputation for himself. In fact, one of his most ardent admirers was the renowned Francis Bacon.

While in London, Anne renewed her friendship with William Hutchinson. About one year following the death of her father, they were married in 1612. Both Anne and her husband were closely following the teachings and sermons of John Cotton. By 1629, the political landscape in England was in a state of flux. King Charles I had dismissed Parliament and was greatly influenced by the Catholic Church. In this political environment, the Puritans felt as if they were under siege once again. This ultimately provoked many Puritans to flee England and gain passage to the New World. Their destination was Plymouth in the Massachusetts Bay Colony that was established in 1620. It was in the year of 1633 that John Cotton moved to Plymouth as well. It was only one year later that Hutchinson left with her family to settle in the New World.

Anne Hutchinson soon organized weekly meetings of local women to discuss recent sermons and to give expression to her own theological views. Before too long, her sessions attracted ministers and magistrates as well. A focal point of her talks was the idea that an individual's intuition served as a means of reaching God and salvation, rather than the observance of institutionalized beliefs and the precepts of ministers. Her opponents accused her of antinomianism—the view that God's grace has freed the Christian from the need to observe established moral precepts. The threat that Hutchinson posed to the established church was twofold. First, this point of view was seen as representing a direct threat to the established hierarchy. Secondly, the idea that these teachings came from an influential, intelligent, and influential woman confounded the local church authorities. She was viewed as an existential threat to the status quo.

Hutchinson's criticism of the Massachusetts Puritans for what she considered to be their narrowly legalistic concept of morality and her protests against the authority of the clergy were at first widely supported by Bostonians in America. John Winthrop, however, opposed her, and she lost much of her support after he won election as governor. She was tried by the General Court chiefly for "traducing the ministers," was convicted in 1637, and was sentenced to banishment. For a time in 1637–38, she was held in custody at the house of Joseph Weld, marshal of Roxbury, Massachusetts. Refusing to recant, she was then tried before the Boston Church and formally excommunicated.

With some of her loyal followers, Hutchinson established a settlement (now Portsmouth) on the island of Aquidneck (now part of Rhode Island) in 1638. After the death of her husband in 1642, she settled on Long Island Sound, near present-day Pelham Bay, New York. In 1643, she and all her servants and children save one were killed by the Siwanoy, an indigenous people of Long Island Sound who reacted violently against white settlers encroaching upon their land. This was an event regarded by some in Massachusetts as a manifestation of divine judgment. In 1987 Massachusetts governor Michael Dukakis officially pardoned Hutchinson.

Anne Hutchinson was an individual who refused to abide by the constraints that were ordinarily placed upon the women of her time. Her independent spirit was, in fact, encouraged and supported by her father.

In spite of the manner in which local authorities both in her native England and in the Massachusetts Bay Colony attempted to suppress her outspokenness, she persisted and became an example of what was possible especially within the so-called *New World*. Anne Hutchinson was one of the earliest examples of an

Joseph Aprile   Anne Hutchinson

outspoken voice for change as expressed by a woman in a time predating by some 150 years the formation of what was to be the Democratic Republic of the United States.

Emma Gotcher

At the turn of the twentieth century, factory workers, in particular, were subject to working conditions that were often inhumane and abysmal. This was in large part due to the unfettered growth and expansion of industrial production in the wake of the so-called, "industrial revolution." The prevalence of this reality of daily life led to social upheavals within human communities due to the fact that living conditions, for many, became unbearable.

Emma Gotcher was sixteen years old when she became embroiled in a case that was brought before the U.S. Supreme Court (Muller v. Oregon (1908) in a suit for greater labor protections. Gotcher worked at Portland's *Grand Laundry* in Oregon. In her time, it was not unusual for woman to work at jobs of this kind for 13 hours per day for a pay that was from 3.50 to 5 dollars per week. In 1902, an Oregon law restricted women from having working days longer than ten hours. This restriction was the first of its kind in Oregon at that time.   This legislation

Joseph Aprile   Emma Gotcher

was regarded as definitive evidence of progress in the eyes of those fighting for labor rights.

Gotcher was born on June 15, 1890 in Wisconsin and married Edward Elmer Gotcher at a young age - little is known of her early years. Her husband was in a leadership role in the Shirtwaist and Laundry Workers' Union. In 1906 some four years after the passage of the Oregon law that restricted working hours for women (as described above), the overseer, Joseph Haselbock, at Emma's place of employment, demanded that she stay beyond ten hours during her shift. Almost immediately, Gotcher reacted by taking her employer to court for failure to comply with Oregon law. The suit was found in her favor and the company was subsequently fined.

Muller, the owner of Portland's Grand Laundry took his complaint to the Oregon Supreme Court, a case that eventually was heard by the U.S. Supreme Court with Melville Fuller as Chief Justice (1888 – 1910). He was represented by William Fenton, a corporate attorney and a well-known defender of corporate interests in regard to labor issues. Fenton cloaked his appeal as being in defense of equal treatment for women under the law.

The Supreme Court at the time was not too accommodating in regard to worker's rights. As a matter of fact, the Lockner v. New York (1905) case had recently ruled in favor of the employer, in this case a bakery, and effectively struck down a similar law in the state of New York claiming that the New York law's limits to working time violated the Fourteenth Amendment - that granted citizenship to all persons born or naturalized in the United States including former enslaved people and guaranteed all citizens "equal protection under the law."

This case involving Gotcher had some notable differences from the Lockner decision that suggested that it might result in a different outcome. It drew the attention of the head of the National Consumers' League (NCL), Florence Kelley, a noted activist for civil rights and women's suffrage causes. The mission of the NCL was to guarantee protections for workers across the country. Kelly hoped to use the national exposure to the plight of Emma Gotcher as a means to a greater end. For this strategy, Kelley won the support of the National Women's Trade Union League.

The NCL hired Louis Brandeis to present the case to the U.S. Supreme Court in defense of the state of Oregon. Brandeis went on to become an Associate Justice of the Supreme Court – appointed by President Woodrow Wilson in 1916 until his retirement in 1939.

Interestingly, Brandeis's strategy was to propose that women had less emotional and physical capacity for day labor than their male counterparts. The defense concluded that protections as outlined in the Oregon statute were necessary in order to protect women's ability to bear children. Of course, such a strategy in the wake of contemporary cultural and social norms would have no reasonable traction. However, during of the time of this case, the social and political environment held full women's civil rights to be controversial - only six states had succeeded in granting women suffrage. In the end, his strategy became successful and Muller lost his appeal.

Once this case was finally settled, Gotcher did not gravitate toward the spotlight and instead retreated into her own private life. At the age of 72-years-old (1962), she died in a car crash along with her husband – they were buried in Lone Fir Pioneer Cemetery in Portland, Oregon. Nonetheless, she left in her wake a significant legacy that set the tone for what was to follow.

Joseph Aprile   Emma Gotcher

By way of further information, Florence Kelley, referred to earlier in this text, died in 1932 before the national legislation passed as a consequence of President Franklin D. Roosevelt's New Deal granted many of the welfare and labor rights that Kelley had worked so hard for.

Anna Arnold Hedgeman

Anna Arnold Hedgeman was born in the late 19th century (1899) in the small town of Marshalltown, Iowa. As a small child, her family moved to Anoka, Minnesota – they were the only black family in their local community. Her parents, William James Arnold II and Marie Ellen (Parker) Arnold, placed a great deal of value and importance upon education and scholarship. They were also active in their community, and Hedgeman did not experience any notable discrimination while growing up. However, she was to feel the full weight of racial prejudice later in her adult life.

Following her graduation in 1918, Hedgeman continued her education at Hamline University In Saint Paul, Minnesota – a private liberal arts college founded in 1854. This university places a strong emphasis on experiential learning, service, and active engagement in issues of social justice.

As a student at the university, she attended a lecture given by Dr. W.E.B. DuBois – a famous sociologist and historian (1868 – 1963) - that she found inspirational and helped direct her aspirations towards a career in education. She graduated from Hamline University in 1922 with a Bachelor of Arts degree in English. She was the first person of color to earn a degree at Hamline University.

One of her first positions post-graduation was a teaching position at Rust College in Holly Springs, Mississippi. Rust College is an historic black college founded in 1866 during the brief period of post-war Reconstruction (1865 – 1877). During her stay in Rust College in the heart of the Deep South she suddenly experienced the full impact of Jim Crow (as discussed previously). She was awakened to this reality even before she arrived in Mississippi by train, for she was obliged to sit in the "colored" car behind the locomotive and was denied access to the dining car on account of the color of her skin as soon as the train departed from the Cairo, Illinois train station.   This demeaning experience sharpened her awareness of the true nature of racism within the United States.

After two years at Rust College, she moved back to Minnesota to find racial barriers confront her when she tried to find a teaching position. In 1924, she accepted a position as executive director of the black branch of the Young Women's Christian Association (YWCA) in Springfield, Ohio; she remained in that position until 1938.

For the following ten years she worked at a number of high-level positions including serving as the Assistant

Dean of Women at Howard University. By 1948, she turned her attention to a political career and worked for the Harry Truman campaign for President of the United States, and went on to become the first black woman to serve on the cabinet of then New York Mayor Robert F. Wagner Jr. In this role, she gained a reputation as a strong advocate for civil rights and was recruited by Philip Randolph and Bayard Rustin to plan and coordinate the 1963 March on Washington that was highlighted earlier in this book (see the chapter devoted to John Lewis).   Serving as the Coordinator of Special Events for the Commission of Religion and Race of the National Council of Churches, Hedgeman convinced some 40,000 Protestants to participate in this march on August 28, 1963, that brought hundreds of thousands of individuals to the nation's capital.

On account of her wide-ranging experience and professional career especially in regard to her inexhaustible advocacy in the area of equal rights for African-Americans, Hedgeman became a sought-after lecturer at black colleges and universities throughout the United States.   She authored a number of books that highlighted her efforts including, *The Trumpet Sounds* (1964) and *The Gift of Chaos* (1977). Hedgeman died on January 7, 1990.

As an African-American woman, Hedgeman came to understand the deleterious impact of racism on the lives of people of color within the United States and dedicated herself to help make substantive changes in this cultural dynamic that remains a persistent aspect of the national landscape.

George Washington Williams

George Washington Williams was born in 1849 in Bedford Springs, Pennsylvania and lived at that residence; until he was fourteen years of age. Although having had no education, he was not lacking in ambition – at the age of fourteen he decided to leave his home and join the Union Army. Having served during the American Civil War (1861 – 1865), he fought in the Mexican War (1867) that ended in the defeat of the Emperor Maximilian, an Austrian archduke. Maximilian's reign was brief (1864 – 1867), and he was summarily executed at the end of the conflict.

Following his military service, Williams focused on getting an education and attended the Newton Theological Institution in Massachusetts. At twenty-five years of age, he became a pastor at the Twelfth Baptist Church in Boston, and by that time he was married. In addition, he was a columnist for the Cincinnati Commercial.

He later became a publisher and founded a local newspaper called *The Commoner* in 1875. He entered the political arena and was elected to the Massachusetts state legislature – the first person of color to achieve this political position. He achieved this office during the brief interval following the American Civil War referred to as Post War Reconstruction (1865 – 1877).

His passion shifted to the study of history. His goal was to include in the history of the United States an assessment of the experiences and contributions to the nation made by African-Americans. As a consequence, his first important treatise was entitled, *The History of the Negro Race in America* in two volumes. This work was generally well received. He also produced a work entitled, *A History of the Negro Troops*.

In 1884, President Chester A Arthur nominated William to fill the post of Ambassador to Haiti. Although the Senate confirmed this position, the incoming Democratic President Grover Cleveland replaced Williams with his own nominee, John Edward Thompson.

In 1890, Williams was assigned by President Benjamin Harrison to study conditions in the Belgian Congo. As a result of his first-hand experience while traveling in the

Congo, he had an opportunity to examine in detail the treatment of the native African population in that region by the Belgian colonialist rulers. He subsequently wrote a letter to the Belgian Crown in which he outlined the appalling conditions that the native peoples had to endure.

The following is the complete text of that letter Williams wrote to King Leopold of Belgium:

"An Open Letter to His Serene Majesty Leopold II, King of the Belgians and Sovereign of the Independent State of Congo By Colonel, The Honorable Geo. W. Williams, of the United States of America," 1890

"Good and Great Friend,

I have the honour to submit for your Majesty's consideration some reflections respecting the Independent State of Congo, based upon a careful study and inspection of the country and character of the personal Government you have established upon the African Continent.

"It afforded me great pleasure to avail myself of the opportunity afforded me last year, of visiting your State in Africa; and how thoroughly I have been disenchanted, disappointed and disheartened, it is now my painful duty to make known to your Majesty in plain but respectful language. Every charge which I am about to bring against your Majesty's personal Government in the Congo has been carefully investigated; a list of competent and veracious witnesses, documents, letters, official records and data has been faithfully prepared, which will be deposited with Her Britannic Majesty's Secretary of State for Foreign Affairs, until such time as an International Commission can be created with power to send for persons and papers, to administer oaths, and attest the truth or falsity of these charges.

"There were instances in which Mr. HENRY M. STANLEY sent one white man, with four or five Zanzibar soldiers, to make treaties with native chiefs. The staple argument was that the white man's heart had grown sick of the wars and rumours of war between one chief and another, between one village and another; that the white man was at peace with his black brother, and desired to "confederate all African tribes" for the general defense and public welfare. All the sleight-of- hand tricks had been carefully rehearsed, and he was now ready for his work. A number of electric batteries had been purchased in London, and when attached to the arm under the coat, communicated with a band of ribbon which passed over the palm of the white brother's hand, and when he gave the black brother a cordial grasp of the hand the black brother was greatly surprised to find his white brother so strong, that he nearly knocked him off his feet in giving him the hand of fellowship. When the native inquired about the disparity of strength between himself and his white brother, he was told that the white man could pull up trees and perform the most prodigious feats of strength. Next came the lens act. The white brother took from his pocket a cigar, carelessly bit off the end, held up his glass to the sun and complaisantly smoked his cigar to the great amazement and terror of his black brother. The white man explained his intimate relation to the sun and declared that if he were to request him to burn up his black brother's village it would be done. The third act was the gun trick. The white man took a percussion cap gun, tore the end of the paper which held the powder to the bullet, and poured the powder and paper into the gun, at the same time slipping the bullet into the sleeve of the left arm. A cap was placed upon the nipple of the gun, and the black brother was implored to step off ten yards and shoot at his white brother to demonstrate his statement that he was a spirit, and, therefore, could not be killed. After much begging the black brother aims the gun at his white brother, pulls the trigger, the gun is discharged, the white man stoops . . . and takes the bullet from his shoe!

"By such means as these, too silly and disgusting to mention, and a few boxes of gin, whole villages have been signed away to your Majesty.

"When I arrived in the Congo, I naturally sought for the results of the brilliant programme: "fostering care", "benevolent enterprise", an "honest and practical effort" to increase the knowledge of the natives "and secure their welfare". 1 had never been able to conceive of Europeans, establishing a government in a tropical country, without building a hospital; and yet from the mouth of the Congo River to its head-waters, here at the seventh cataract, a distance of 1,448 miles, there is not a solitary hospital for Europeans, and only three sheds for sick Africans in the service of the State, not fit to be occupied by a horse. Sick sailors frequently die on board their vessels at Banana Point; and if it were not for the humanity of the Dutch Trading Company at that place—who have often opened their private hospital to the sick of other countries—many more might die. There is not a single chaplain in the employ of your Majesty's Government to console the sick or bury the dead. Your white men sicken and die in their quarters or on the caravan road, and seldom have Christian burial. With few exceptions, the surgeons of your Majesty's Government have been gentlemen of professional ability, devoted to duty, but usually left with few medical stores and no quarters in which to treat their patients. The African soldiers and labourers of your Majesty's Government fare worse than the whites, because they have poorer quarters, quite as bad as those of the natives; and in the sheds, called hospitals, they languish upon a bed of bamboo poles without blankets, pillows or any food different from that served to them when well, rice and fish.

"I was anxious to see to what extent the natives had "adopted the fostering care" of your Majesty's "benevolent enterprise" (?), and I was doomed to bitter disappointment. Instead of the natives of the Congo "adopting the fostering care" of your Majesty's Government, they everywhere complain that their land has been taken from them by force; that the Government is cruel and arbitrary and declare that they neither love nor respect the Government and its flag. Your Majesty's Government has sequestered their land, burned their towns, stolen their property, enslaved their women and children, and committed other crimes too numerous to mention in detail. It is natural that they everywhere shrink from "the fostering care" your Majesty's Government so eagerly proffers them.

"There has been, to my absolute knowledge, no "honest and practical effort made to increase their knowledge and secure their welfare." Your Majesty's Government has never spent one franc for educational purposes, nor instituted any practical system of industrialism. Indeed the most unpractical measures have been adopted against the natives in nearly every respect; and in the capital of your Majesty's Government at Boma there is not a native employed. The labour system is radically unpractical; the soldiers and labourers of your Majesty's Government are very largely imported from Zanzibar at a cost of £10 per capita, and from Sierra Leone, Liberia, Accra and Lagos at from £1 to £1/10 per capita. These recruits are transported under circumstances more cruel than cattle in European countries. They eat their rice twice a day by the use of their fingers; they often thirst for water when the season is dry; they are exposed to the heat and rain, and sleep upon the damp and filthy decks of the vessels often so closely crowded as to lie in human ordure. And, of course, many die.

"Upon the arrival of the survivors in the Congo they are set to work as labourers at one shilling a day; as soldiers they are promised sixteen shillings per month, in English money, but are usually paid off in cheap handkerchiefs and poisonous gin. The cruel and unjust treatment to which these people are subjected breaks the spirits of many of them, makes them distrust and despise your Majesty's Government. They are enemies, not patriots.

"There are from sixty to seventy officers of the Belgian army in the service of your Majesty's Government in the Congo of whom only about thirty are at their post; the other half are in Belgium on furlough. These officers draw double pay—as soldiers and as civilians. It is not my duty to criticise the unlawful and unconstitutional use of these officers coming into the service of this African State. Such criticism will come with more grace from some Belgian statesman, who may remember that there is no constitutional or organic relation subsisting between his Government and the purely personal and absolute monarchy your Majesty has established in Africa. But I take the liberty to say that many of these officers are too young and inexperienced to be entrusted with the difficult work of dealing with native races. They are ignorant of native character, lack wisdom, justice, fortitude and patience. They have estranged the natives from your Majesty's Government, have sown the seed of discord between tribes and villages, and some of them have stained the uniform of the Belgian officer with murder, arson and robbery. Other officers have served the State faithfully, and deserve well of their Royal Master.

"From these general observations I wish now to pass to specific charges against your Majesty's Government.

"FIRST.—Your Majesty's Government is deficient in the moral military and financial strength, necessary to govern a territory o 1,508,000 square miles, 7,251 miles of navigation, and 31,694 square miles of lake surface. In the Lower Congo River there is but One post, in the cataract region one. From Leopoldville to N'Gombe, a distance of more than 300 miles, there is not a single soldier or civilian. Not one out of every twenty State-officials know the language of the natives, although they are constantly issuing laws, difficult even for Europeans, and expect the natives to comprehend and obey them. Cruelties of the most astounding character are practised by the natives, such as burying slaves alive in the grave of a dead chief, cutting off the heads of captured warriors in native combats, and no effort is put forth by your Majesty's Government to prevent them. Between 800 and 1,000 slaves are sold to be eaten by the natives of the Congo State annually; and slave raids, accomplished by the most cruel and murderous agencies, are carried on within the territorial limits of your Majesty's Government which is impotent. There are only 2,300 soldiers in the Congo.

"SECOND.—Your Majesty's Government has established nearly fifty posts, consisting of from two to eight mercenary slave-soldiers from the East Coast. There is no white commissioned officer at these posts; they are in charge of the black Zanzibar soldiers, and the State expects them not only to sustain themselves, but to raid enough to feed the garrisons where the white men are stationed. These piratical, buccaneering posts compel the natives to furnish them with fish, goats, fowls, and vegetables at the mouths of their muskets; and whenever the natives refuse to feed these vampires, they report to the main station and white officers come with an expeditionary force and burn away the homes of the natives. These black soldiers, many of whom are slaves, exercise the power of life and death.

They are ignorant and cruel, because they do not comprehend the natives; they are imposed upon them by the State. They make no report as to the number of robberies they commit, or the number of lives they take; they are only required to subsist upon the natives and thus relieve your Majesty's Government of the cost of feeding them. They are the greatest curse the country suffers now.

"THIRD.—Your Majesty's Government is guilty of violating its contracts made with its soldiers, mechanics and workmen, many of whom are subjects of other Governments. Their letters never reach home.

"FOURTH.—The Courts of your Majesty's Government are abortive, unjust, partial and delinquent. I have personally witnessed and examined their clumsy operations. The laws printed and circulated in Europe "for the Protection of the blacks" in the Congo, are a dead letter and a fraud. T have heard an officer of the Belgian Army pleading the cause of a white man of low degree who had been guilty of beating and stabbing a black man, and urging race distinctions and prejudices as good and sufficient reasons why his client should be adjudged innocent. I know of prisoners remaining in custody for six and ten months because they were not judged. T saw the white servant of the Governor-General, CAMILLE JANSSEN, detected in stealing a bottle of wine from a hotel table. A few hours later the Procurer-General searched his room and found many more stolen bottles of wine and other things, not the property of servants. No one can be prosecuted in the State of Congo without an order of the Governor-General, and as he refused to allow his servant to be arrested, nothing could be done. The black servants in the hotel, where the wine had been stolen, had been often accused and beaten for these thefts, and now they were glad to be vindicated. But to the surprise of every honest man, the thief was sheltered by the Governor General of your Majesty's Government.

"FIFTH—Your Majesty's Government is excessively cruel to its prisoners, condemning them, for the slightest offences, to the chain gang, the like of which can not be seen in any other Government in the civilized or uncivilized world. Often these ox-chains eat into the necks of the prisoners and produce sores about which the flies circle, aggravating the running wound; so the prisoner is constantly worried. These poor creatures are frequently beaten with a dried piece of hippopotamus skin, called a "chicote", and usually the blood flows at every stroke when well laid on. But the cruelties visited upon soldiers and workmen are not to be compared with the sufferings of the poor natives who, upon the slightest pretext, are thrust into the wretched prisons here in the Upper River. I cannot deal with the dimensions of these prisons in this letter, but will do so in my report to my Government.

"SIXTH.—Women are imported into your Majesty's Government for immoral purposes. They are introduced by two methods, viz., black men are dispatched to the Portuguese coast where they engage these women as mistresses of white men, who pay to the procurer a monthly sum. The other method is by capturing native women and condemning them to seven years' servitude for some imaginary crime against the State with which the villages of these women are charged. The State then hires these woman out to the highest bidder, the officers having the first choice and then the men. Whenever children are born of such relations, the State maintains that the women being its property the child belongs to it also. Not long ago a Belgian trader had a child by a slave-woman of the State, and he tried to secure possession of it that he might educate it, but the Chief of the Station where he resided, refused to be moved by his entreaties. At length he appealed to the Governor-General, and he gave him the woman and thus the trader obtained the child also. This was, however, an unusual case of generosity and clemency; and there is only one post that I know of where there is not to be found children of the civil and military officers of your Majesty's Government abandoned to degradation; white men bringing their own flesh and blood under the lash of a most cruel master, the State of Congo.

"SEVENTH.—Your Majesty's Government is engaged in trade and commerce, competing with the organised trade companies of Belgium, England, France, Portugal and Holland. It taxes all trading companies and exempts its own goods from export-duty, and makes many of its officers ivory-traders, with the promise of a liberal commission upon all they can buy or get for the State. State soldiers patrol many villages forbidding the natives to trade with any person but a State official, and when the natives refuse to accept the price of the State, their goods are seized by the Government that promised them "protection". When natives have persisted in trading with the trade-companies the State has punished their independence by burning the villages in the vicinity of the trading houses and driving the natives away.

"EIGHTH.—Your Majesty's Government has violated the General Act of the Conference of Berlin by firing upon native canoes; by confiscating the property of natives; by intimidating native traders, and preventing them from trading with white trading companies; by quartering troops in native villages when there is no war; by causing vessels bound from "Stanley-Pool" to "Stanley-Falls", to break their journey and leave the Congo, ascend the Aruhwimi river to Basoko, to be visited and show their papers; by forbidding a mission steamer to fly its national flag without permission from a local Government; by permitting the natives to carry on the slave- trade, and by engaging in the wholesale and retail slave-trade itself.

"NINTH.—-Your Majesty's Government has been, and is now, guilty of waging unjust and cruel wars against natives, with the hope of securing slaves and women, to minister to the behests of the officers of your Government. In such slave-hunting raids one village is armed by the State against the other, and the force thus secured is incorporated with the regular troops. I have no adequate terms with which to depict to your Majesty the brutal acts of your soldiers upon such raids as these. The soldiers who open the combat are usually the bloodthirsty cannibalistic Bangalas, who give no quarter to the aged grandmother or nursing child at the breast of its mother. There are instances in which they have brought the heads of their victims to their white officers on the expeditionary steamers, and afterwards eaten the bodies of slain children. In one war two Belgian Army officers saw, from the deck of their steamer, a native in a canoe some distance away. He was not a combatant and was ignorant of the conflict in progress upon the shore, some distance away. The officers made a wager of £5 that they could hit the native with their rifles. Three shots were fired and the native fell dead, pierced through the head, and the trade canoe was transformed into a funeral barge and floated silently down the river.

"TENTH.—Your Majesty's Government is engaged in the slave-trade, wholesale and retail. It buys and sells and steals slaves. Your Majesty's Government gives £3 per head for able bodied slaves for military service. Officers at the chief stations get the men and receive the money when they are transferred to the State; but there are some middle-men who only get from twenty to twenty-five francs per head. Three hundred and sixteen slaves were sent down the river recently, and others are to follow. These poor natives are sent hundreds of miles away from their villages, to serve among other natives whose language they do not know. When these men run away a reward of 1,000 N'taka is offered. Not long ago such a recaptured slave was given one hundred "chikote" each day until he died. Three hundred N'taka—brassrod-—is the price the State pays for a slave, when bought from a native. The labour force at the stations of your Majesty's Government in the Upper River is composed of slaves of all ages and both sexes.

"ELEVENTH.—Your Majesty's Government has concluded a contract with the Arab Governor at this place for the establishment of a line of military posts from the

Seventh Cataract to Lake Tanganyika territory to which your Majesty has no more legal claim, than I have to be Commander-in-Chief of the Belgian army. For this work the Arab Governor is to receive five hundred stands of arms, five thousand kegs of powder, and £20,000 sterling, to he paid in several instalments. As I write, the news reaches me that these much- treasured and long-looked for materials of war are to be discharged at Basoko, and the Resident here is to be given the discretion as to the distribution of them. There is a feeling of deep discontent among the Arabs here, and they seem to feel that they are being trifled with. As to the significance of this move Europe and America can judge without any comment from me, especially England.

"TWELFTH—The agents of your Majesty's Government have misrepresented the Congo country and the Congo railway. Mr. H. M. STANLEY, the man who was your chief agent in setting up your authority in this country, has grossly misrepresented the character of the country. Instead of it being fertile and productive it is sterile and unproductive. The natives can scarcely subsist upon the vegetable life produced in some parts of the country. Nor will this condition of affairs change until the native shall have been taught by the European the dignity, utility and blessing of labour. There is no improvement among the natives, because there is an impassable gulf between them and your Majesty's Government, a gulf which can never be bridged. HENRY M. STANLEY'S name produces a shudder among this simple folk when mentioned; they remember his broken promises, his copious profanity, his hot temper, his heavy blows, his severe and rigorous measures, by which they were mulcted of their lands. His last appearance in the Congo produced a profound sensation among them, when he led 500 Zanzibar soldiers with 300 camp followers on his way to relieve EMIN PASHA. They thought it meant complete subjugation, and they fled in confusion. But the only thing they found in the wake of his march was misery. No white man commanded his rear column, and his troops were allowed to straggle, sicken and die; and their bones were scattered over more than two hundred miles of territory.

"CONCLUSIONS

"Against the deceit, fraud, robberies, arson, murder, slave-raiding, and general policy of cruelty of your Majesty's Government to the natives, stands their record of unexampled patience, long-suffering and forgiving spirit, which put the boasted civilisation and professed religion of your Majesty's Government to the blush. During thirteen years only one white man has lost his life by the hands of the natives, and only two white men have been killed in the Congo. Major Barttelot was shot by a Zanzibar soldier, and the captain of a Belgian trading-boat was the victim of his own rash and unjust treatment of a native chief.

"All the crimes perpetrated in the Congo have been done in your name, and you must answer at the bar of Public Sentiment for the misgovernment of a people, whose lives and fortunes were entrusted to you by the august Conference of Berlin, 1884—1 885. I now appeal to the Powers which committed this infant State to your Majesty's charge, and to the great States which gave it international being; and whose majestic law you have scorned and trampled upon, to call and create an International Commission to investigate the charges herein preferred in the name of Humanity, Commerce, Constitutional Government and Christian Civilisation.

"I base this appeal upon the terms of Article 36 of Chapter VII of the General Act of the Conference of Berlin, in which that august assembly of Sovereign States reserved to themselves the right "to introduce into it later and by common accord the modifications or ameliorations, the utility of which may be demonstrated experience".

"I appeal to the Belgian people and to their Constitutional Government, so proud of its traditions, replete with the song and story of its champions of human liberty, and so jealous of its present position in the sisterhood of European States—to cleanse itself from the imputation of the crimes with which your Majesty's personal State of Congo is polluted.

"I appeal to Anti-Slavery Societies in all parts of Christendom, to Philanthropists, Christians, Statesmen, and to the great mass of people everywhere, to call upon the Governments of Europe, to hasten the close of the tragedy your Majesty's unlimited Monarchy is enacting in the Congo.

"I appeal to our Heavenly Father, whose service is perfect love, in witness of the purity of my motives and the integrity of my aims; and to history and mankind I appeal for the demonstration and vindication of the truthfulness of the charge I have herein briefly outlined.

"And all this upon the word of honour of a gentleman, I subscribe myself your Majesty's humble and obedient servant,

GEO. W. WILLIAMS
Stanley Falls, Central Africa,
July 18th, 1890."

Williams was hoping that the publication of this letter would inspire a protest movement that would hopefully address his detailed concerns. He was disappointed by the lack of meaningful response. He subsequently moved to England to work on a book with a focus on Africa. Unfortunately, he fell seriously ill shortly after his arrival and died at the young age of 41.

Given his austere beginnings and apparent lack of formal education, Williams' achievements were extraordinary especially considering the fact that he was an African-American who grew up and developed within the United States during an era when his people were sorely oppressed. Much of his life's work was dedicated to leaving a significant historic record in regard to the injustices imposed upon people of color not only in the United States but also to Africans within their own homelands. He was highly intelligent, caring, well-disciplined, and utilized his many abilities and talents to contribute a great deal to the life of the nation. He made a valiant effort to awaken the nation to its momentous failings.

Mathew Ahmann

Mathew Ahmann worked closely with key players in the Civil Rights Movement during the 1960's including Dr. Martin Luther King Jr. He had a major role in the planning and implementation of the March on Washington for Jobs and Freedom on August 28, 1963, and was one of leaders of the procession from the Washington Monument to the Lincoln Memorial where King delivered his historic address.

At that time Ahmann, thirty-one years of age, was the founding director of the National Catholic Conference for Interracial Justice (NCCIJ). An important aspect of Ahmann's work in regard to the NCCIJ was to promote its activities and services in regard to issues of social and economic justice for racial and ethnic minorities.

The following is the full text of the letter from Ahmann to Paul Tanner, Catholic Bishop of St. Augustine, Florida, in which he asked for both moral and financial support for the social justice undertaking of the NCCIJ.

"It was encouraging to read of the recent formation of the national conference of Catholic Bishops. It was even more encouraging, for us at the national Catholic Conference for Interracial Justice, to read your statement on race relations and poverty. We thank you sincerely for this statement, particularly for the concrete way in which the grave needs of minority Americans were expressed. Since 1960 our conference has labored to produce and make available specific, workable programs to respond to the needs you enunciated, "reducing principles to action ideals to programs". We are the only national Catholic service agency working full time in race relations.

"As emphasized in your statement, now is the time to increase Catholic leadership in the critical areas of equal housing, jobs and education. Our conference offers tested programs, a professional staff, and experience in working with local and national relations agencies. There are almost 150 local Catholic human relations organizations alone to which we direct our services.

"It was especially gratifying to read your forthright endorsement of affirmative action by employers and unions to secure fully integrated working forces. Project Equality, initiated and serviced by this Conference, is the nation's largest private program to achieve this goal; with the cooperation of over 12,000 firms, Project Equality now operates in 43 religious jurisdictions- Catholic dioceses and Protestant, Orthodox and Jewish bodies.

"At this critical time, we appeal to you and your diocese for a measure of concrete support for our programs. There has been a heavy increase in requests for our services, and we ask your financial help to strengthen these services- in employment, education, medical care, aids to pastors, urban affairs (this last a newly organized project) and to support our efforts to shape new programs and services which are both specific and workable. We enclose a brief summary of various conference programs.

"Thank you very much.

Sincerely yours,
Mathew Ahmann
Executive Director."

Mathew Ahmann was born on September 10, 1931, in St. Cloud, Minnesota. His father, Norbert Ahmann was a dentist and his mother, Clotilda Ahmann. a nurse. He was the oldest of three brothers; Catholicism played a major role in their upbringing with a strong emphasis placed upon the value of hard work, education, and public service.

Ahmann graduated in 1952 with a degree in the social sciences at St. John's University and from there went on to graduate studies at the University of Chicago. As a graduate student, he became so involved in the Civil Rights Movement that he dropped out of the graduate program.

In Chicago, he worked for several years as the director of the Chicago Catholic Interracial Council. He founded and became the director of the NCCIJ. One of his first major projects as director was to organize the National Conference on Religion and Race that convened on January 14, 1963 and ended on January 17. He specifically scheduled it to coincide with 100th anniversary of the Emancipation Proclamation (1863) issued by President Abraham Lincoln that called an end to the institution of slavery. Ahmann claimed his goal for the conference was to, "examine the role of religious institutions and then move on to propose and inspire renewed action and interreligious projects to increase the leadership of religion in ending racial discrimination."

With Ahmann's passion for social justice and his apparent mastery of organizational skills, he was asked by the organizers of the March on Washington for Jobs and Freedom to find a Catholic Bishop who would be willing to serve as the Catholic chairman for the march. After repeated attempts to do so, he was unable to accomplish this. Instead, he volunteered to join the organizing committee and make an introductory speech at the march. He was joined by A. Philip Randolph, John L. Lewis, Reverend Eugene Carson, Walter Reuther, Floyd McKissick, Whitney Young, Roy Wilkins, and Rabbi Joachim Prinz.

The following is an excerpt from that speech,

"We are gathered a long 100 years after Lincoln declared slavery at an end in the United States. Yet, slavery is all too close to us as we demonstrate for equality and freedom today...we have permitted racial discrimination to remain with us too long...But we are gathered ...to dedicate ourselves to building a people, a nation, a world which is free...of discrimination based on race, creed, color or national origin... There is no turning back." It was at this march, that Dr. Martin Luther King Jr. gave his famous *I Have a Dream* speech.

Following this historic event, Ahmann broadened his focus to include women's rights. He worked with the NCCIJ until 1968. In 1969 he relocated to Texas where he took on the job of director of the Commission on Church and Society for the Archdiocese of San Antonio. For sixteen years, he worked as the associate director for Catholic Charities USA in Washington D.C. He also served as an executive committee member of the Leadership Conference on Civil and Human Rights.

Ahmann died of cancer on December 31, 2001. Although never in the spotlight, he had an illustrious career as an activist and organizer that exposed his unrelenting passion for civil and human rights spanning many decades.

Jacinda Ardern

Jacinda Ardern is the current Prime Minister of New Zealand. During her time in office, she has faced many challenges even in such a small country as New Zealand. Currently, of course, Ardern is confronted by the global COVID-19 pandemic that remains prevalent around the world and has taken the lives of over 5.4 million individuals as of January 2022. In addition to this global crisis, on *March 15, 2019, New Zealand was faced with an horrendous episode of domestic terrorism - the mass shooting of Muslims near their place of worship. At that time, Ardern exhibited a presence of mind and a will to effective action that was both inspired and memorable.

Ardern was born July 26, 1980 in Hamilton, New Zealand, and spent her childhood in the small farming town of Murupara in a rural environment on New Zealand's North Island. As a child in that environment, she grew up helping to tend the farm – operating farm machinery, tending to sheep and harvesting fruit.

Eventually, the family moved north to the Bay of Plenty. In that more urban setting, Ardern became exposed to the realities of social and economic inequality that informed her and help shape her future goals.

According to her, "I always noticed when things felt unfair. Of course, when you're a kid, you don't call it social justice. I just thought it was wrong that other kids didn't have what I had."

This reality, encouraged her to engage in activities that sought to effect change. Ardern was inspired to join human rights groups at school. One of these efforts involved campaigning for young women to be allowed to wear long pants as an acceptable part of the traditional school uniform at her school, Morrinsville College. The efforts of this work proved successful.

In 2005, she went on an extended trip to the UK. This kind of journey was rather commonplace for her age – New Zealand is part of the United Kingdom's (UK) Commonwealth of Nations. There she worked in the cabinet office of then Prime Minister Tony Blair where her primary responsibility was to determine ways in which local civil authority could improve its relationship with small businesses.

In 2007, she was elect president of the International Union of Socialist Youth (IUSY).   This gave her the opportunity to travel to Algeria, China, India, Israel, Jordan, and London.   Undoubtedly, through this experience, she had an opportunity to make direct contact with a variety of cultures and gained access to a broader perspective regarding governance.

On October of 2017, she became New Zealand's 40th Prime Minister (PM) after having become the leader of the Labour Party in August of that year.   In her leadership role as New Zealand's PM, Ardern was regarded as a strong advocate of women's rights.   However her support of human rights went beyond gender and extended to all the people of New Zealand that she represented as the nation's political leader.   This expansive view was made abundantly clear in the aftermath of the horrific mass shooting that occurred at a mosque in Christchurch New Zealand in March of 2019.   In response to this tragedy Ardern said, "They were New Zealanders.   They are us.   And because they are us, we, as a nation, mourn them."   She condemned the attacker while choosing to avoid using his name and subsequently moved to propose stricter gun laws.

On account of the grievous nature of this tragedy, Ardern addressed the nation in the following way, "While we are at home with more than two hundred ethnicities, that does not mean we are free from racism and discrimination.   We have wounds from our own history that, two hundred and fifty years on from the first encounters between Maori and Europeans, we continue to address. But since the terrorist attack in New Zealand, we have had to ask ourselves many hard and difficult questions."

Within ten days of the attack, the gun laws were significantly modified, and military-style weaponry was effectively banned in New Zealand.

This horrific event occurred only one short year before the COVID-19 global pandemic struck New Zealand. Attentive to the devastation this virus visited on other countries, Ardern focused her attention towards implementing a policy that involved closing the nation's borders and mandated a month-long nationwide shutdown as a means to prevent the unbridled dissemination of the virus throughout the population. She remained mindful, however, of the sacrifice she was asking of her people. Ardern called upon everyone to work together and show compassion towards others.

In her words, "We're all now putting each other first, and that is what we do so well as a nation. So, New Zealand be calm, be kind, stay at home and break the chain." As a result, New Zealand experienced one of the lowest death rates per million people in the midst of the global pandemic.

Ardern has repeatedly shown through her style of leadership a determined desire to address national issues such as homelessness, child poverty, the inadequacies of the nation's mental health system and climate change.

Climate change represents a formidable challenge that threatens the viability of the human species for the long term. As a result of Ardern's commitment to addressing this issue, the New Zealand Parliament passed historic legislation in November of 2019 that is projected to reduce the nation's carbon emissions to zero by the year 2050.

As Prime Minister, Ardern has demonstrated the effectiveness of her approach and has clearly shown that compassion and a genuine concern for the general welfare of her countrymen are effective tools to implement substantial, progressive and meaningful change.

Chief Raoni Metuktire

Chief Raoni Metuktire is the chief of the Kayapo people who populate a region of the Amazon Rain Forest. It is this vast region in South America that represents a highly important resource that plays a central role in the stability of the global climate especially with the added threat of climate change that is a direct consequence of human activity.

The Amazon Rain Forest has been threatened for decades due to the unabated incursion of commercial development that has had a devastating impact on the the region – threatening the delicate ecological balance that sustains this natural system. As a result, the livelihood, safety, and security of the indigenous peoples that populate this region have been under continuous assault.

Chief Raoni has been involved in the preservation of the remaining rain forest that is home to his people for decades and has repeatedly risked his own safety in the pursuit of this elusive goal. Although there is no official record of his birth, it has been assumed that he was born around 1932 in a village called

Krajmopyjakare, otherwise known as Kapot. This village resides in the midst of the region referred to as the Mato Grosso in Brazil (see map below).

The Kayapo are a nomadic people; as a child he lived in many locations. At the age of 15, Raoni participated in the rites of initiation as a warrior and wore a labret – an ornamental disk placed in his lower lip and that was gradually replaced by larger disks. It took four months for his lower lip to reach its current size.

In 1954, Raoni met the Villas Broas brothers – Orlando, Claudio and Leonardi were Brazilian activists that drew attention to the plight of the indigenous people of Brazil and ultimately succeeded in getting the upper Xingu legally protected. He stayed with them for a year, learned Portuguese and was greatly influenced by their outlook and energetic activism.

Joseph Aprile   Chief Raoni Metuktire

It was in 1973 that Chief Raoni began a friendship with noted French film maker, Jean Pierre Dutilleux, that ultimately led to the release of a documentary film entitled *Raoni* that was presented at the 1977 Cannes festival. This gave Chief Raoni and the plight of his people worldwide exposure. He used this publicity as an opportunity to highlight the threat that unrestricted deforestation posed upon the rain forest ecosystem and the survival of the indigenous populations that lived within these forests.

In 1989, Chief Raoni enlisted the help of Sting, a popular British rock band to broadcast his message. It was the first time he ever traveled beyond his homeland of Brazil. The resulting impact of all these activities aroused enough global support that a vast tropical reservation was created in 1993 that encompassed the Mato Grosso and Para states in Brazil. In addition, Chief Raoni won the support of such notable individuals as French President, Mitterrand and the former French President Chirac, The king of Spain, Juan Carlos, and Pope John Paul II.

Chief Raoni Metuktire remains a charismatic and influential leader in support of the indigenous peoples of the rain forest and an outspoken proponent of a sustainable planet.

Summary and Conclusion

Faced with the ever-growing list of highly problematic issues that face humanity and its future prospects in the 21st century, there is the very human tendency to retreat into a state of consciousness that resides within the protective boundaries of denial. This mindset not only obscures the real status of human existence in the modern era, but also creates in its stead a picture of the world that is filled with rich and vibrant color, luxurious and comforting textures and, most importantly, an exaggerated image of self that speaks of grand and extravagant possibilities.

Modern humans have become so effectively isolated and separated from the natural world, the environment of our collective origin as a species, that we are thoroughly imbedded in a human-crafted environment that relies upon artificial and often fanciful constructs. The concepts imprinted within the thinking brain holding such a distorted perspective, reveal a universe where wealth and its accumulation consume much of human endeavor; where pleasure, comfort, convenience and personal happiness are regarded with so much more importance than the health and longevity of the human species and other life forms on the planet, and where many of the images that constantly impinge upon the human retina have their origins in completely artificial and contrived sources and are often quite meaningless in content.

The sum total of these influences has created a social order that is predicated upon a complex and interlaced set of delusional elements. As a result, modern humans move about their world in a near-constant state of distraction. In such a state, human behavior continues to unravel and undermine the future security and viability of the species. In such a state, pre-occupation with self and its shallow pursuits seem to subsume all other considerations.

Despite the ingenuity and richness of this delusional world, the real nature of existence remains unabetted. The future that awaits humanity is a natural consequence of all the choices we make and continue to make in the present time. To ignore this fundamental reality is to consign ourselves to a future that may prove quite unfavorable to humanity's continued existence.

The individuals referred to in this volume, represent a collective voice that calls us to break free from this delusional world we have created concerning the nature of reality and awaken to the global issues of peace and social justice that still haunt the fabric of human societies and human endeavor. These voices remind us of the necessity of finding peaceful and workable solutions to the problems that have arisen as a result of the cumulative impact and consequences of human behavior. Otherwise, we will forever be haunted by the past and perpetuate the cycle of violence and retribution that has stymied human progress for so long.

We have looked at historic figures like Anne Hutchinson, George Washington Williams, Dame Cecile Saunders and Chief Joseph of the Nez Perce in the United States who put down his weapons and spoke eloquently regarding the plight of his people in the face of the colonial expansion of white settlers into the homeland of his nation and the need for peace. Other indigenous leaders we have examined include Sarah Deer, Maxima Acuna De Chapeu, Elouise P Cobell, and Cecile Ann Hansen.

We have looked at the courageous work of the Civil Rights Movement in the United States in the 1960s under the guidance of individuals like John Lewis, and Mathew Ahmann who willingly and repeatedly risked their personal safety to secure social justice for African-Americans

We have examined the life of Fred Korematsu and Gordon Hirabayashi who courageously took a stand in refusing to comply to the order No. 9066 that precipitated the forced internment of Japanese-Americans during World War II. They have since been honored for their remarkable tenacity in the face of such repression.

We have studied the actions of Nadia Murad Basee Taha, in opposition to the brutal and murderous treatment of her people, the Yazidi people from Northern Iraq, under the relentless assault by ISIS, and Rose Mapendo from the Democratic Republic of the Congo as examples of courageous outspoken voices in defense of regional human rights. In this same light we have focused on the remarkable courage of Raif Badawi who has faced imprisonment and possible execution for his open opposition to the repressive government of Saudi Arabia.

We have learned of remarkable tenacity of Chief Raoni Metuktire of the Kayopo people in The Amazon Rain Forest who reminded the world of the disastrous impact of commercial exploitation of pristine regions of the planet by the powerful on the lives and livelihoods of native peoples who legitimately fear extinction.

We have referred to some of the insightful words and actions of Arthur Waskow and his wife Helen Berman who have been unshakeable advocates of global peace and social justice. They have both transcended their regional affiliation with the State of Israel and have been tireless in their efforts to encourage peaceful solutions to seemingly intractable human problems

Finally, we have highlighted contemporary political leaders like, Stacey Abrams, Pramila Jayapal, and Jacunda Adern, Prime Minister of New Zealand, as examples of forward-looking, inclusive, and progressive governance.

The human world is currently immersed in a crisis that is unlike any humanity has faced since Homo sapiens had its beginnings in Africa when the species diverged from its common ancestor with the chimpanzee some six million years ago. Although many human civilizations have experienced dramatic ascents and precipitous and catastrophic collapses over the thousands of years of ancient and modern history, those calamities were felt locally. Notable examples of these were the disintegration of the Roman Empire in the fifth century AD and the fall of the Soviet Empire in the twentieth century. Currently, however, the species faces dire prospects for the future that have ramifications on a global scale to the extent that the viability of the entire species may be at stake.

Since the end of the last ice age (approximately 11700 years ago), human societies and cultures have enjoyed a relatively stable planetary environment – the global climate has been moderate enough to allow for substantial and steady progress in advances of civilization especially in the areas of science and technology. This has allowed humans to grow in numbers to the current population estimated to be 7.9 billion individuals. It has been the general assumption, until relatively recently, that this moderate global environment would persist indefinitely into the future.

This assumption, however, is in serious conflict with the onset of climate change unfolding as a direct result of the kinds of human activities that, ironically, have made the life we have come to know possible. The dawn of the machine age – around the early 18th century with the invention of the steam engine – effectively supplanted human labor with energy-hungry machines and allowed for the accelerated growth and expansion of human civilizations.

The study of the past has shown that the planet has endured at least five catastrophic epochs that produced massive extinctions of species around the world - the latest occurring some 60 million years resulting in the eradication of the dinosaurs. Each of these protracted periods of time were accompanied by a dramatic change in climatic conditions that proved fatal for vast multitudes of species. The recovery from these events took many thousands of years.

In the twenty-first century humanity faces the prospect of yet another calamitous global epoch. This time, however, climate change is occurring due to the ever-increasing accumulation of greenhouse gases in the atmosphere as a direct result of human activity. Already the collective impact of climate change is being felt worldwide. This reality has inspired some anthropologists to suggest that the name of the current epoch be changed from Holocene to Anthropocene to reflect the full extent of the human impact on the global environment.

Even with this knowledge in-hand, humanity has failed to respond to the extent that would have any meaningful impact upon an ominous unfolding of events. Any real corrective change in human behavior obviously requires a global commitment. In a sense, the real progression of historic events will be a testimonial to the level of fitness of the species required to endure, overcome, and forestall this pending crisis. To date the species is failing this test.

One just needs to examine the evidence across the planet to see the grim picture that awaits us all. In the

United States we have a cacophony of discordant voices that are chaotic, unfocused, and dismissive in regard to the magnitude of the problem that confronts us. In Brazil, we have those in power who are determined to denude vast stretches of the Amazon Rain Forest – a vital global carbon sink – for the purpose of economic gain at the expense of the viability of local indigenous peoples and future human generations on a global scale. In the Middle East – an area of the globe in which human beings may soon be unable to live due to the projected increase in ambient temperature – needless violence and reckless aggression is continuing over relatively minor differences in religious beliefs and customs. Russia – a vast territory - continues to depend upon the export of fossil fuels for its economic well-being. Many countries in Africa are beset by a level of societal chaos – often inflamed by religious differences – that makes any focused attention to the problem of climate change nearly impossible. India and Pakistan remain embroiled in endless confrontation fueled once again over religious differences this time between Hindu and Muslim. Together these two countries account for over 1.3 billion individuals.

In effect, the human species seems unable to break free from behaviors that have their origin in the realm of unchecked emotions and essentially tribal, cultural, political, and religious affiliations. As a result, a considerable portion of the wealth of economic resources throughout the world is devoted to developing technologies for military purposes. The net impact of these actions is to significantly diminish the level of commitment and global cooperation absolutely required to effectively halt or mitigate the apparent inevitability of dramatic changes in earth's climate.

In addition to the shadow cast by the prospects of climate change, the year 2020 has been in many ways disturbing and unsettling. What, of course, comes to mind is the COVID-19 pandemic that has claimed so many lives and has been economically devastating to many facets of the global economy, especially for those who have lost their livelihoods and businesses. Added to this worldwide burden are the inherent fractures that have been exposed in regard to deep-seated issues of peace and social injustice that continue to haunt human societies around the globe.

Along with this overwhelming sense of loss, however, is the untold bravery, courage and unwavering energy displayed by so many who have risked their own lives and safety to come to the aid of all of us for the unselfish commitment to the greater good. These individuals have come from many diverse positions - as doctors, nurses, emergency response teams, members of the police and fire departments and first responders of all kinds. To this list, we should include all those responsible for providing food; for delivering the mail; for the taxi and bus drivers, train operators and pilots; for the teachers; for all those who care for the elderly, and for all those who provide the essential services that we all too often take for granted.

Taking all these factors into consideration, the human species has the unprecedented opportunity to grow wiser from the events that have befallen us and see the future as a time for healing and learning from our collective missteps. This could be a time of new beginnings. It is imperative that we finally come to recognize that regardless of our national origin, religious affiliation, skin color or sexual orientation we are all members of the same species with the same physical bodies, the same architecture of the brain, the same genetic makeup, and the same constellation of feelings, of hopes and of dreams. Each of us is worthy of the same opportunities to grow and develop as sentient beings on this most remarkable planet that also needs our kindness, care, and attention. Earth is, after all, our only home. We can fashion a social order focused upon creating a sane, intelligent, and sustainable future for ourselves and future generations.

References

Arthur Waskow
Arthur Waskow, *Dancing in God's Earthquake: the Coming Transformation of Religion*, Orbis Books, 2020

Arthur Waskow, *The Rest of Creation*, Albion-Andalus Books, 2016

Phyllis Berman
Sojourners, *Rabbi Phyllis Berman,*
https://sojo.net/biography/rabbi-phyllis-berman, 2018

Join the World Biographical Encyclopedia, *Phyllis Ocean Berman,*
https://prabook.com/web/phyllis_ocean.berman/677758, 2018

Phyllis Ocean Berman, *A Time for Every Purpose Under Heaven*, Farrar, Straus and Giroux, 2003

Walt and Milly Woodward
Mary Woodward and David Guterson, *In Defense of Neighbors: the Walt and Milly Story*, Fenwick, 2008

William Wilberforce
Eric Metaxas, *Amazing Grace: William Wilberforce and the Heroic Campaign to End Slavery*, HarperOne, 2007

William Wilberforce (Author) and Bob Beltz (Editor): *Real Christianity,* Bentley House Publishers, 2006

Nadia Murad Basee Taha
Nadia Murad, *The Last Girl: My Story of Captivity and My Fight Against the Islamic State*, Tim Duggan Books, 2017

Nadia Murad Nobel Lecture (2018)
https://www.nobelprize.org/prizes/peace/2018/murad/lecture

Rose Mapendo
Beth Davenport and Elizabeth Mandel, *Pushing the Elephant,* Film, 2010

Elouise P Cobell
Truth to Power, YouTube video, https://www.youtube.com/watch?v=fKbDZQGfDq0, 2008

Oscar Arias Sanchez
Oscar Arias Sanchez, *Bringing Peace to Central America*, Chelsea House Publications, 2007

Oscar Arias Sanchez Nobel Peace Prize (1987) - https://www.nobelprize.org/prizes/peace/1987/arias/facts/, 1987

Denis Mukwege Mukengere
Denis Mukwege Nobel Lecture (2018)
https://www.nobelprize.org/prizes/peace/2018/mukwege/55721-denis-mukwege-nobel-lecture-2/, 2018

Maxima Acuna De Chaupeu
The Goldman Environmental Prize, *"Maxima Acuna – 2016 Goldman Prize Recipient South and Central America"*,

https://www.goldmanprize.org/recipient/maxima-acuna/, 2016

Cecile Ann Hansen
Peter Blecha, *Hansen, Cecile: Tribal Chairwoman of Seattle's Duwamish Peoples*, *https://www.historylink.org/File/8963*, 2009

Pramila Jayapal
Clare Foran, *Pramila Jayapal is one of the most powerful leaders on Capitol Hill*, *https://www.cnn.com/2021/10/30/politics/who-is-pramila-jayapal/index.html*

Pramila Jayapal, *Pilgrimage to India: A Woman Revisits her Homeland*, Basic Books, 2001

Pramila Jayapal, *Use the Power You Have: A Brown Woman's Guide to Politics and Political Change*, The New Press, 2020

Fred Korematsu
Smithsonian Magazine, *Erick Trickey Fred Korematsu Fought Against Japanese Internment in the Supreme Court...and Lost*, https://www.smithsonianmag.com/history/fred-korematsu-fought-against-japanese-internment-supreme-court-and-lost-180961967/ , 2017

Gordon Hirabayashi
Gordon H. Hirabayashi, *A Principled Stand – The Story of Hirabayashi V. United States*, University of Washington Press, 2013

University Libraries, Northwest Historical Document Collection, *Gordon K. Hirabayashi letter entitled, Why I Refused to Register for Evacuation, May 13,1942,* https://digitalcollections.lib.washington.edu/digital/collect ion/pioneerlife/id/21356/

John Lewis
Jon Meacham, *His Truth is Marching On – John Lewis and the Power of Hope*, Merewether LLC, 2020

Chief Joseph of the Nez Perce
Kent Newburn, *Chief Joseph & the Flight of the Nez Perce*, HarperOne, 2005

Stacey Abrams
Stacey Abrams, *Lead from the Outside: How to Build your Future and Make Real Change*, Henry Holt and Co., 2018

Raif Badawi
Raif Badawi, *1000 lashes Because I Say What I Think*, Constantin Schreiber et al, 2015

Ensaf Haidar and Andrea Claudia Hoffmann, *The Voice of Freedom: My Husband, Our Story*, Other Press, 2016

Sarah Deer
Sarah Deer, *"The Beginning and End of Rape: Confronting Sexual Violence in Native America"*, University of Minnesota Press, 2015

The City University of New York, May 29, 2020, "Brooklyn College Celebrates the Class of 2020 Through Virtual Celebration", https://www1.cuny.edu/mu/forum/2020/05/29/brooklyn-college-celebrates-class-of-2020-through-virtual-celebration/

Dame Cicely Saunders
Dame Cicely Saunders,, *Hospice and Palliative Care: An Interdisciplinary Approach*, Arnold Publishers, 1990

Norman Autton and Dame Cicely Saunders, *Pain an Exploration*, Danton, Longman and Todd Ltd., 1986

Anne Hutchinson
Eve LaPlante, *"American Jezebel: The Uncommon Life of Anne Hutchinson, the Woman who Defied the Puritans"*, HarperOne, 2009

Captivating History, *Anne Hutchinson: A Captivating Guide to the Puritan Leader in Colonial Massachusetts who is Considered to be One of the Earliest American Feminists*, 2020

Emma Gotcher
Metro News Quinn Spencer, *Emma Gotcher fighter for labor rights*, https://www.oregonmetro.gov/news/emma-gotcher-fighter-labor-rights, 2021

Anna Arnold Hedgeman
Jennifer Scanlin, *Until There is Justice; The Life of Ann Arnold Hedgeman*, Oxford University Press, 2016

National Women's History Museum Emma Rothberg, *Anna Arnold Hedgeman,* https://www.womenshistory.org/education-resources/biographies/anna-arnold-hedgeman

George Washington Williams
O'Connor, A. (2008, January 23). *George Washington Williams (1849-1891),* https://www.blackpast.org/african-american-history/williams-george-washington-1849-1891

John Hope Franklin, George Washington Williams (Chicago: University of Chicago Press, 1985); Clyde N. Wilson, ed., American Historians, 1866-1912 (Detroit: Edwards Brothers, Inc., 1986), Linda Heywood, Allison Blakely, Charles Stith, and Joshua C. Yesnowitz, eds.,

John Hope Franklin. *George Washington Williams: A Biography*, The University of Chicago Press, 1985

George Washington Williams Jr, George Washington Williams, *A History of the Negro Race in America from 1619 – 1880 Volume and Negro as Slaves, as Soldiers and as Citizens"*, 2012

George Washington Williams and John David Smith, *A History of the Negro Troops in the War of the Rebellion, 1861-1865 (The North's Civil War

Mathew Ahmann
Mathew Ahmann, *The New Nego: Edited by Mathew Ahmann; Co-Contributors Steven Wright [And Others] in the Symposium James Baldwin and Others,* Notre Dame Ind.: Fides Publishers, 1961

Jacinda Ardern

Jacinda Ardern, *I Know this to be True*, Blackwell&Ruth, 2020

Chief Raoni Metuktire

Walter R. Echo-Hawk and Araya S Jones, *In the Light of Justice: The Rise of Human Rights and UN Declaration on the Rights of Indigenous Peoples*, Fulcrum Publishing, 2013

The Guardian, *Amazonian Chief Raoni Metuktire; 'Bolsonaro has been the worst for us'*, the guardian.com https://www.theguardian.com/world/2020/jan/02/amazonian-chief-raoni-metuktire-bolsonaro-has-been-the-worst-for-us, 2020

Matthieu Bonnet, 2021, Chief Raoni Metuktire Biography, raoni.com, http://raoni.com/biography.php, 2021

Index

www.ingramcontent.com/pod-product-compliance
Lightning Source LLC
Chambersburg PA
CBHW061516120726
48001CB00004B/1338